WARRIOR • 136

CHINDIT 1942–45

TIM MOREMAN   ILLUSTRATED BY PETER DENNIS

Series editors Marcus Cowper and Nikolai Bogdanovic

First published in Great Britain in 2009 by Osprey Publishing
Midland House, West Way, Botley, Oxford, OX2 0PH, UK
443 Park Avenue South, New York, NY 10016, USA
E-mail: info@ospreypublishing.com

A CIP catalogue record for this book is available from the British Library

ISBN: 978-1-84603-373-5
E-Book ISBN: 978-1-84603-882-2

Editorial by Ilios Publishing, Oxford, UK (www.iliospublishing.com)
Cartography by Bounford.com
Page layout by Mark Holt
Index by Alan Thatcher
Typeset in Sabon and Myriad Pro
Originated by PPS Grasmere Ltd., Leeds, UK
Printed in China through Worldprint Ltd

09 10 11 12 13   10 9 8 7 6 5 4 3 2 1

FOR A CATALOGUE OF ALL BOOKS PUBLISHED BY OSPREY MILITARY
AND AVIATION PLEASE CONTACT:

NORTH AMERICA
Osprey Direct, c/o Random House Distribution Center, 400 Hahn Road,
Westminster, MD 21157
Email: uscustomerservice@ospreypublishing.com

ALL OTHER REGIONS
Osprey Direct, The Book Service Ltd, Distribution Centre, Colchester Road,
Frating Green, Colchester, Essex, CO7 7DW
E-mail: customerservice@ospreypublishing.com

www.ospreypublishing.com

Osprey Publishing are supporting the Woodland Trust, the UK's leading
woodland conservation charity, by funding the dedication of trees.

ACKNOWLEDGMENTS

The author is indebted to David Grant, Brian Nicholls and Ann Hunter
of the British Mule Society. Thanks are also due to Alan Jeffreys at the
Imperial War Museum.

ARTIST'S NOTE

Readers may care to note that the original paintings from which the
colour plates in this book were prepared are available for private sale.
The Publishers retain all reproduction copyright whatsoever. All enquiries
should be addressed to:

Peter Dennis
Fieldhead,
The Park,
Mansfield,
Nottinghamshire NG18 2AT
UK

The Publishers regret that they can enter into no correspondence
upon this matter.

IMPERIAL WAR MUSEUM COLLECTIONS

Many of the photos in this book come from the Imperial War Museum's
huge collections which cover all aspects of conflict involving Britain
and the Commonwealth since the start of the twentieth century.
These rich resources are available online to search, browse and buy at
www.iwmcollections.org.uk. In addition to Collections Online, you can
visit the Visitor Rooms where you can explore over 8 million photographs,
thousands of hours of moving images, the largest sound archive of its
kind in the world, thousands of diaries and letters written by people
in wartime, and a huge reference library. To make an appointment,
call (020) 7416 5320, or e-mail mail@iwm.org.uk.
Imperial War Museum www.iwm.org.uk

ABBREVIATIONS

AA	Anti-aircraft
AT	Anti-tank
CO	Commanding officer
DF	Defensive fire
ECO	Emergency commissioned officer
fps	feet per second
GHQ India	General Headquarters, India
GCO	Gurkha commissioned officers
GR	Gurkha Rifles
HE	High explosive
IJA	Imperial Japanese Army
LMG	Light machine gun
LRP	Long-range penetration
LRPG	Long Range Penetration Group
MMG	Medium machine gun
NCO	Non commissioned officer
OR	Other ranks
SAA	Small-arms ammunition
SMG	Submachine gun
SMLE	Short Magazine Lee-Enfield
US	United States
USAAF	United States Army Air Force
VCO	Viceroy commissioned officers

CONTENTS

CHINDIT 1942–45

INTRODUCTION – THE CHINDITS AND ORDE WINGATE

The Chindits – the brainchild of the idiosyncratic Major-General Orde Wingate, who went on to lead them in battle in Japanese-occupied Burma between 1942 and 1944 – were arguably the most controversial body of fighting men raised by Great Britain during World War II. Named after a mispronunciation of the Burmese word *Chinthe*, the mythical half lions/half dragons that guarded temples and monasteries in Burma, this specially organized, trained and equipped body of men employed innovative fighting methods based on ideas originally developed by its commander in Palestine and Ethiopia. This new approach to war fighting was dubbed long-range penetration (LRP), in which lightly armed and equipped troops, operating without conventional artillery, tank and logistical support, carried out offensive operations deep in the jungle behind enemy lines with the aim of collecting intelligence, cutting enemy lines of communication, disrupting command and control, attacking base installations and diverting troops from other tasks. To accomplish this essentially guerrilla mission, Long Range Penetration Groups (LRPGs), using radios for air–ground communication, were supplied by transport aircraft, dispensing with fixed lines of communication, and were given close air support by fighters and bombers in lieu of normal artillery.

Long-range penetration was tested experimentally by the Chindits against the Imperial Japanese Army during Operation *Longcloth* between February and May 1943, when 77th Indian Infantry Brigade, composed of British, Gurkha and Burmese troops, marched cross-country from Manipur into central Burma through Japanese lines. A series of hit-and-run raids were successfully carried out in the Japanese rear areas by small columns of troops, briefly interdicting the rail network, before the exhausted survivors marched to safety, covering over 1,000 miles on foot. Despite having suffered heavy losses to enemy action, tropical disease and the hot and humid climate, and having achieved little of lasting military significance, on their return the Chindits were lionized by the British press desperate to report a success in Burma, where hitherto the Japanese had been in the ascendant. As a result Operation *Longcloth* was trumpeted worldwide as a physical and psychological victory over the jungle and the Japanese.

The Chindits – given the name Special Force or 3rd (Indian) Division as a security measure – underwent massive expansion in size during the summer and autumn of 1944, with powerful personal support from Prime Minister

Winston Churchill (frustrated by lack of progress in South-East Asia) and the Combined Chiefs of Staff easing the way. It was achieved primarily by breaking up the conventional British 70th Division and creaming off the best manpower from other units, despite vehement opposition from critics in India Command who regarded it as a diversion from the main war effort and a misuse of highly trained troops. Eventually six LRP brigades were raised for operations in Northern Burma in 1944 along with a separate organization for their administration, supply and training. A lavish scale of arms, and new equipment, moreover, was made available in quantities hitherto unknown in the Far East. To facilitate operations, the US authorities also placed No. 1 Air Commando at Special Force's disposal, which was equipped with US Army Air Force (USAAF) light aircraft, transport and close-support aircraft and also briefly the US 5307th Composite Unit (Provisional) – better known as Merrill's Marauders – to be trained in LRP. Overall the expansion of Special Force entailed a massive increase in status for Wingate, who had never so much as commanded a battalion in battle and had now suddenly taken charge of what was in reality a small corps. A period of intensive training was carried out in Central India and the tactics of LRP further refined based on combat experience gained during 1943. Henceforward, instead of small striking columns roving over the countryside, fortified 'strongholds' would be constructed at key points in the jungle that the Japanese would have to attack in strength.

Special Force was flown into battle in Northern Burma on 5 March 1944 over 200 miles behind enemy lines by transport aircraft or glider, with the exception of 16th Brigade, which marched overland from Ledo to Indaw. Unfortunately Major-General Orde Wingate died in an air crash in Manipur on 23 March, leaving the Chindits bereft of his leadership. For the next five months its officers and men, deployed in brigade-sized Long Range Penetration Groups, fought under appalling climatic conditions deep in the jungle, in operations

The Dakota transport aircraft, flown by both the US Army Air Forces and Royal Air Force, was the workhouse used to re-supply the Chindits throughout Operation *Thursday.* (IND 5277)

A group of Chindits on Operation *Longcloth* prepare a railway bridge for demolition. (SE 7921)

increasingly of a more conventional nature. Under the command of Major-General 'Joe' Lentaigne, they were committed to heavy fighting in Northern Burma in support of US and Chinese forces, increasingly using methods very different from those devised by Wingate. In August 1944 they were finally withdrawn to India, but by then they were a pale shadow of their former selves, thanks to battle casualties, tropical disease and general debilitation caused by fighting during the monsoon. A period of rest, recuperation and retraining immediately began, but early in 1945 the Chindits were summarily disbanded and their officers and men redistributed throughout South-East Asia Command.

The short lifespan of the Chindits was marked by controversy. Both at the time and ever since, the actual contribution they made in the final balance to Allied victory in the Far East has been debated with considerable acrimony. A large part of their notoriety stems from Major-General Orde Wingate himself, whose enigmatic personality, military ideas and controversial style of leadership brought him into conflict with senior officers. Instead of revisiting these debates in any depth, however, this book will examine the officers, NCOs and men who proudly wore the Chinthe badge and carried out some of the most difficult operations of World War II. Undoubtedly they make for a worthy subject, given the fearsome opponent they fought and the difficulties of climate and terrain they overcame. Following intensive specialized training, the Chindits fought long, hard campaigns, living, moving and fighting against the Imperial Japanese Army deep in the Burmese jungle, suffering considerable hardship. Heavy losses were inflicted in the process from enemy action, the hostile climate and disease, since they were retained in the fighting line long after it had been planned they should be withdrawn for rest and recuperation. In the process the Chindits won four Victoria Crosses as well as a wide range of other awards for gallantry.

CHRONOLOGY

1941
7 December   Outbreak of World War II in the Far East.

1942
16 January   Japanese invade Burma.

27 January   Colonel Orde Wingate meets Wavell in New Delhi.

March–April   Brigadier Orde Wingate arrives in Burma and carries out a reconnaissance.

End of May   Remnants of Burcorps reach Imphal.

June–July   Wavell agrees to test Long Range Penetration, and 77th Indian Infantry Brigade is formed. It begins training at Saugor in the Central Provinces.

1943
14 February   Operation *Longcloth* begins.

March   77th Indian Infantry Brigade crosses the Irrawaddy River.

26 March   Wingate orders withdrawal to India.

18 April   Chindits re-cross the Irrawaddy River.

28 April   Wingate and his dispersal party cross the Chindwin River.

May–June   The survivors of Operation *Longcloth* return to Assam in dribs and drabs.

October   Authority granted to raise a new enlarged Chindit force known as Special Force or 3rd (Indian) Division.

1944
5 February   Operation *Thursday* begins. 16th Brigade leaves Ledo to march 600 miles to Indaw on foot.

5 March   16th Brigade crosses the Chindwin River.

5/6 March   The lead elements of 77th Indian Infantry Brigade are flown in to Broadway. Build up of Broadway begins.

6/7 March   Lead gliders land at Chowringhee followed by two battalions of 111th Indian Infantry Brigade.

Lieutenant George Cairns, Somerset Light Infantry, attached to 1st South Staffordshire Regiment, who was awarded a posthumous Victoria Cross early during Operation *Thursday*. (HU 2052)

7 March	Stilwell's Chinese Armies advance down the Hukawaung and Mogaung valleys.
15 March	Japanese Offensive on Imphal Plain and Kohima begins.
16 March	77th Indian Infantry Brigade reaches Mawlu and constructs White City.
20 March	16th Brigade begins work on Aberdeen stronghold.
24 March	Major-General Orde Wingate dies in a plane crash in Assam
24 March	16th Brigade attacks Indaw and is later repulsed.
27 March	Major-General W.D.A. Lentaigne takes command of the Chindits.
27 March	Broadway comes under Japanese attack.
6 April	Japanese commence a series of fierce attacks on White City.
April	14th Brigade lands at Aberdeen and attacks a series of Japanese supply dumps.
17 April	Japanese make last attack on White City.
27 April	16th brigade captures Indaw East airfield, but it is quickly abandoned after demolition work is completed.
7/8 May	Blackpool is occupied by 111th Indian Infantry Brigade.
9/10 May	White City is evacuated. Its garrison is moved north.
11 May	Broadway is abandoned. Its garrison is moved north.
16/17 May	Slim formally hands over command of the Chindits to Stillwell.
25 May	A defeated and exhausted 111th Brigade abandons Blackpool.
6 June	77th Brigade begins its attack on Mogaung.
26 June	Chindits capture Mogaung.
June	The 14th, 3rd West African and 111th brigades continue operations near Hill 60, Shmaw and Point 2171.
27 August	The last Chindits (77th, 14th and 3rd West African brigades) are evacuated to India.

1945
22 January	Burma Road re-opens.
February	The Chindits are disbanded.

No. 10119 Rifleman Tulbahadur
Pun, 6th Gurkha Rifles, who
was awarded a Victoria Cross
for bravery during the fighting
at Mogaung on 23 June 1944.
(MH 2606)

RECRUITMENT

The Chindits never had a formal recruitment or selection procedure akin to
other Special Forces with which they have erroneously been identified. Instead,
in accordance with Wingate's deeply held belief that any 'ordinary' solder could
be trained to operate behind enemy lines using LRP methods, conventional
units were simply allotted by GHQ India to this highly specialized role. As
Wingate wrote shortly before Operation *Longcloth* began:

> If ordinary family men from Liverpool and Manchester can be trained for this
> specialized jungle war behind the enemy's lines, then any fit man in the British
> Army can be trained to do the same, and we show ourselves to the world as
> fighting men second to none, which I believe we are. (*Burchett 1944, p.179*)

Those troops originally selected for 77th Indian Infantry Brigade, for example, were a very mixed bag. By far the best and most experienced (veterans of the retreat from Burma) were the men of 142nd Commando Company led by Major Michael Calvert, intended to provide demolition teams, and the 2nd Burma Rifles, organized in reconnaissance platoons, whose Chins, Karens and Kachins acted as guides, scouts and interpreters. The bulk of the units selected for Operation *Longcloth* – the only ones available in 1942, comprising the 13th King's (Liverpool) Regiment and 3/2nd Gurkha Rifles – were hardly from the 'First Eleven', with a high proportion of highly inexperienced and very old or very young men filling the ranks. The 13th King's (Liverpool) Regiment had been raised only for coastal defence duties in the UK and then sent to carry out internal security in India. The average age of its mostly married men was 33, but all had completed basic training. In comparison the green 3/2nd Gurkha Rifles was filled with recruits of just 11 months' military experience – mostly just 18 – who volunteered to serve as part of the Indian Army following its massive expansion in the wake of the outbreak of World War II. A shortage of Gurkhali-speaking British officers compounded the problem and many of these young, inexperienced British ECOs were not enamoured by Wingate or his ideas.

The Chindits may have recruited ordinary line battalions, but all were subjected to a rigorous weeding out process to fit them for the task that lay ahead. A gruelling training regime (discussed later in this book) quickly removed physically and psychologically unfit officers, non-commissioned officers (NCOs) and other ranks (ORs) deemed unsuitable for arduous and particularly stressful service behind enemy lines. This included all men over 40 years of age, including many commanding officers (COs) and field grade officers, judged incapable of carrying out LRP duties by virtue of age. To fill gaps opened by such wastage, volunteers were accepted from units all over India Command, including officers and men to fill specialist posts. While most were good, some units seized the opportunity to rid themselves of shirkers and the unfit.

CHINDIT MULE LEADER

A large part of each Chindit column consisted of 'First Line' mules carrying heavier weapons and ammunition used by fighting troops and 'Second Line' animals carrying radios, ammunition and other stores needed on campaign. Last and by no means least, mules provided a source of (albeit unpalatable) food on the hoof when required. Given their obvious importance the welfare of mules was always of vital importance, with particular care exercised by animal transport officers and muleteers to keep them fit and well despite the rigours of a jungle campaign. Heavy losses, however, were suffered from disease and injuries inflicted by poorly packed or balanced loads that rubbed their backs sore. As always, mules proved particularly vulnerable to enemy action, however, with many dying from Japanese shellfire in strongholds during Operation *Thursday* since it proved difficult to adequately protect them below ground level. The men of mule transport platoons played a vital role in 1943–44, responsible for leading, feeding and caring for their charges. It was an often dangerous, arduous and frequently thankless task. Each mule leader was responsible for one animal and its saddle, with his duties including feeding, washing and grooming each animal, keeping its equipment clean, seeing that its load was properly tied and balanced, stopping animals becoming galled, broken winded or lost, hauling the mule to its feet when it fell, and keeping it quiet and under control when in nightly bivouacs. Paradoxically perhaps during Operation *Longcloth*, however, few of the Gurkhas chosen to look after these animals had had much instruction, being hurriedly collected from Gurkha battalions throughout India Command and receiving very little training in animal husbandry before being committed to battle. The upshot of this was heavy losses during the campaign, which in itself hamstrung further operations.

A bearded Chindit leads a heavily encumbered mule through the Burmese jungle. (SE 7910)

The expansion of the Chindits from a single brigade to over a divisional-sized formation saw no radical departure in recruitment patterns for what was now known as Special Force. While the remaining fit troops of 77th Indian Infantry Brigade formed a hard core, new units were allocated during 1942 first to make up 111th Indian Infantry Brigade. The bulk of the infantry for Operation *Thursday*, however, was drawn from regular battalions of 70th Division, despite strong opposition from GHQ India that wanted to keep this British infantry division in being. In addition, Wingate was allocated the as yet raw and untried troops of 3rd West African Brigade. All these troops were in a very different league from the low-quality troops of his first brigade. 70th Division was composed of crack, battle-hardened and highly trained conventional troops. Even so, its constituent units did not escape weeding out during an extremely arduous training period, which again winnowed out the wheat from the chaff, in addition to those simply judged too old for the operations ahead at the grand age of 40 as before. Gaps again were filled by volunteers from all over India Command.

TACTICS AND TRAINING

The tactical doctrine devised by Wingate for waging hit-and-run guerrilla warfare behind Japanese lines, exploiting the Chindits' mobility and ability to evade enemy pursuit by hiding in the vastness of the Burmese jungle, was very different from that used by conventional British and Indian units in the Far East. To carry out this highly specialized role major changes were necessary in the organization, equipment and armament of Chindit units, which in turn influenced their tactical handling and training.

The 400-man strong 'column' (built around an infantry company of three platoons) became the main sub-unit in combat, with eight initially formed in the first LRP brigade. Each column consisted of a headquarters, a Burma Rifles reconnaissance platoon, a demolition or commando squad, an infantry company of four platoons, a support platoon equipped with two 3-inch mortars and two Vickers medium machine guns (MMGs), a mule transport platoon, an air liaison detachment composed of an RAF officer and radio operators, a doctor and two orderlies and a radio detachment for intercommunication. A hundred mules provided first- and second-line transport and 15 horses mounts for officers. Bullocks also accompanied 77th Indian Infantry Brigade on Operation *Longcloth*, as well as the occasional 'liberated' elephant. Given the Chindits' reliance on air supply the Royal Air Force section, equipped with radios carried on mule back, was vital and had responsibility for arranging supply drops, directing the construction of emergency airstrips and directing close air support sorties from the ground. On campaign each column normally operated independently, marching through the jungle, making hit-and-run and attacks and then dispersing as required to avoid enemy attacks to reform at pre-arranged rendezvous points. Occasionally columns would combine with one or more other units for a specific operation.

The selected units of 77th Indian Infantry Brigade deployed to a training area at Saugor, near Jhansi, in the Central Provinces in July 1942, where the monsoon had just broken, with units occupying bivouacs far from nearby roads deep in the dripping wet scrub jungle. This area had been deliberately chosen for its resemblance to central Burma, where the brigade was destined to operate. A comprehensive and particularly gruelling training regimen immediately began, personally devised by Wingate, who believed hard training was the key to success, despite the appalling weather that flooded bivouacs and drowned several

A Royal Air Force sergeant operates an air–ground wireless set in a jungle bivouac. (IND 2292)

men. A constant stream of pamphlets, training instructions and other directives were promulgated by Brigade HQ, complementing a series of lively lectures, group discussions and Tactical Exercises Without Troops given by Wingate expounding his still developing ideas about LRP in the jungle.

The level of training and combat effectiveness of units assigned to Wingate was very mixed. As already noted, while the 142nd Commando Company and the 2nd Burma Rifles were highly trained and experienced, the rest were not. Indeed, the majority of 77th Indian Infantry Brigade needed remedial basic work in addition to specialized instruction in the tactics of LRP before being judged ready for combat. The 13th King's (Liverpool) Regiment and 3/2nd Gurkha Rifles contained a high proportion of inexperienced, very old or very young soldiers in its ranks, possessing only a sketchy knowledge of individual military skills and minor tactics inculcated during basic training; considerable work was needed to make them fit for combat. On top of this, weapons training and training for specialists – signallers, Vickers MMG crews and mortar crews – was urgently required, and this continued throughout the training period. This was not an isolated phenomenon. A major training deficit existed throughout India Command

A radio operator uses a No. 22 set to maintain contact between Chindit columns. (IND 2074)

as a result of the massive expansion of the pre-war Indian Army, battle losses in Malaya and Burma and a lack of experienced officers to command and train the plethora of units.

The new Chindits had first to learn to live and move through the jungle – a key lesson of the retreat from Burma – absorbing such skills as jungle lore (identifying edible/harmful plants and building shelters). This included long periods of time simply accustomizing them to the sights and sounds of the jungle by day and night, which for most was a strange, depressing and frightening environment, as well as learning how to move quickly and quietly through

B **ORDE WINGATE SUPERVISING TRAINING**

Major-General Orde Wingate was arguably one of the most eccentric British officers to reach high command during World War II. His experience of guerrilla warfare in Palestine and Ethiopia had marked him out as a gifted leader of irregular troops, and based upon this impressive record General Wavell brought him to India Command in 1942 to apply his ideas to the war against the Imperial Japanese Army in Burma. As the originator of long-range penetration, he was keenly interested in directing and overseeing the instruction of British, Gurkha, West African and Burmese troops that came under his command between 1942 and 1944. His standards were always high, and those who failed to meet them often fell victim to his violent temper. Training continued right up to the last minute before troops were committed to Operation *Thursday*, with the late arrivals to Special Force in particular still having much to learn about living, moving and fighting in the jungle in accordance with the specialized principles and tactics of long-range penetration. In this illustration Wingate is shown at Lalaghat in Assam in March 1944, as Chindits embarked upon Waco gliders and Dakota transport aircraft (many for the first time), which can be seen in the background.

difficult terrain. In particular, the vital skills needed to live, move and fight in the jungle included map reading, jungle navigation, scouting and patrolling, and marksmanship also received attention.

Training overseen by Wingate consisted primarily of long series of forced marches, by day or night, carrying full arms, ammunition and equipment through the surrounding jungle, often on short common rations and without adequate water. These marches, moreover, inculcated skills such as silent movement, and compass and map reading in jungle terrain, as well as building up the necessary physical and mental stamina required by men carrying heavy packs for extended periods of time. This relentless training proved particularly arduous, especially for officers and men who had enjoyed a 'soft' war to date, with many pushed beyond the limits of what they thought they could endure. As a result the ranks were heavily thinned to remove the unfit and those who fervently wished themselves elsewhere. Training during the monsoon months in itself caused casualties from disease, with dysentery and malaria abounding. Within three weeks of training commencing, 30 per cent of the British battalion was either in or trying to enter hospital. A peak figure of 70 per cent on sick parade was reached four weeks later, but this was reduced so that at the end of training it stood at just three per cent. New blood was injected into units by selecting officers, NCOs and volunteers from other units serving in India Command, who arrived in dribs and drabs throughout the training period.

The new and highly specialized tactics of LRP were carefully gradually inculcated to all ranks in a system of progressive training, working first as sections and platoons and ultimately as columns, once troops became accustomed to the jungle. LRP tactics were broken down into simple stages and taught as drills that were practised incessantly until they became almost second nature. These included marching in 'column snakes' through different types of jungle, 'jigs' to disguise a path taken and confuse a pursuing enemy, crossing open spaces, dispersal drills carried out on unexpected contact with the enemy or after a raid before reassembling at a remote location, and moving into and out of bivouacs. The latter covered the procedure for columns moving quickly into and out of designated bivouac areas, occupying a defensive position, unloading mules and then building fires, cooking food and constructing shelters. Particular drills were also developed for immediate action and contact with the enemy, covering attacking villages, patrolling, constructing booby traps and establishing ambushes and blocks. River crossings were also regularly practised in Central India. A long series of exercises were also carried out simulating attacks on airfields, demolition of bridges and laying various types of ambushes on enemy lines of communication.

The pack mule was a vital part of the Chindits. Indeed, without them long-range penetration would have been impossible, since the mule was the only form of transport capable of negotiating the jungle and indeed of going almost anywhere a man could go without him having to use his hands. The long trains of mule transport accompanying each Chindit column were, however, often a tactical liability; they required careful protection, since the loss of even a few animals could have disastrous results. Mules were often very difficult, moreover, to conceal. Indeed, before Operation *Thursday* mules were 'de-voiced' by Royal Army Veterinary Corps or Indian Army Veterinary Corps vets to prevent mules braying and betraying the position of Chindit columns to the enemy. This hardy, sure-footed and stoic beast of burden, a valued and often dearly loved companion to many Chindits, was employed for a variety of tasks.

The fact that each Chindit column was dependent on mules for transportation and aircraft for re-supply meant careful training in both areas was essential. The training of RAF and Army personnel in the intricacies of air supply – completely new to all – was vital given its centrality to Wingate's ideas of LRP. This included selecting drop zones, clearing vegetation as required and building signal fires, radio and visual signalling to aircraft, gathering parachuted and free-dropped supplies and then quickly distributing it to individual men. Aircraft to train with, however, were in very short supply. In particular, the new Chindits also had much to learn about handling mules and animal husbandry in general. Most of the newly designated muleteers had no experience whatsoever of pack animals, upon which columns depended for

A US Army engineer uses a grader, landed by glider, to level an airstrip in Burma to make it suitable for transport aircraft. (SE 7932)

first- and second-line transport. The former carried support weapons, heavy wireless sets, ammunition and spare light machine guns (LMGs), while the latter carried spare bedding, rations and other vital equipment. Loading and unloading was carefully practised, as well as care of the animals, who could easily suffer galls from chafing of badly packed or poorly balanced loads.

77th Indian Infantry Brigade's training culminated in a brigade-level exercise with all columns simulating an attack on Jhansi, after marching over 180 miles on foot, just before Christmas 1942. Much had been achieved in hardening the troops and teaching them LRP. As Philip Stibbe recalled:

> We all knew how to live and move in the jungle; we all had a pretty good idea of the special tactics we were going to employ and every man in the column had some idea about how to use a map and compass, a skill which was later to save many lives.' (*Stibbe 1994, p.25*)

With hindsight, however, it is clear that the basic military skills of many of Wingate's troops remained poor, which later caused serious difficulties throughout Operation *Longcloth*. Insufficient attention, moreover, had been paid to swimming, river crossings and watermanship. The fault for failing to remedy these serious problems must lie at Wingate's door, since he had six months' grace and full responsibility for instruction. Overall combat effectiveness was further undermined by the last-minute arrival of individual junior officers, muleteers and infantry drafts in the effort to make up numbers.

Training for Operation *Longcloth* and Operation *Thursday*

The experience gained during Operation *Longcloth* taught much about the specialized tactics of LRP and living, moving and fighting in the jungle against the Imperial Japanese Army. These lessons were quickly passed on in training to 111th Indian Infantry Brigade (already under training) and then from October 1943 the rest of the now greatly expanded and newly dubbed Special

Force (or 3rd Indian Infantry Division). These new Chindits faced an uphill task, since just 20 weeks were allocated to reorganizing and converting them to this demanding new role. While the basic training regimen for LRP followed at Saugor was retained and implemented, there were several important differences in that followed between 1943 and 1944. The size of Special Force, and the fact that for much of time he was seriously ill with typhoid, meant that Wingate could not personally supervise instruction. Even so he poured out training instructions. In his stead officers who had fought on Operation *Longcloth* filled command appointments and acted as instructors. For example, Brigadier Bernard Fergusson ran a series of cadres for new column commanders in 70th Division. A newly raised Special Force Training and Experimental Wing also assisted by training instructors in LRP, as well as developing methods for employing new equipment. A major difference was that the majority of troops preparing for Operation *Thursday* were very different in terms of quality to those allocated before. Those drawn from 70th Division, for example, were already highly trained and had had prior combat experience in North Africa. Many units had also carried out prior jungle training since arriving in India Command. Last and by no means least, arms and equipment were available on a scale unknown the year before, in particular aircraft.

A Chindit column fords a shallow river during the early stages of Operation *Thursday*. Two Burmese rafts are in the foreground. (IND 2290)

Training carried out by Special Force at Jhansi in Uttar Pradesh and Gwalior in Madhya Pradesh, after the necessary major reorganization and re-equipment

had been carried out, generally followed three themes: developing physical fitness and endurance, general jungle training and then the study of the tactics of LRP. Increasingly the latter consisted of a blend of guerrilla and conventional fighting methods, with a resulting different emphasis occurring within Special Force itself as commanders trained and later fought in accordance with their own ideas. New tactics had also to be learnt, particularly the 'stronghold' concept introduced by Wingate at the very last minute before Operation *Thursday* began. Instead of just employing hit-and-run methods, it was intended that Chindit columns would occupy strong defensive positions at key sites and draw Japanese attacks upon themselves that could be defeated in detail by dug-in infantry, artillery and airpower.

The Chindits carried out a further extended period of training to teach troops to live, move and fight in the jungle, including further instruction in jungle craft and jungle lore. A long series of gruelling, forced cross-country marches through the jungle, often carrying over 70 pounds of weapons, ammunition and equipment, were carried out, building both physical endurance and mental toughness. Simultaneously they were introduced to LRP tactics during static individual and collective instruction, column marches and frequent exercises. Training covered making bivouacs, river crossings, demolitions, laying ambushes and using explosives, as well as map-reading

JUNGLE TACTICS

The tactics of long-range penetration were highly specialized, and throughout the Chindits' comparatively brief existence were almost constantly being refined and updated by their originator – Major-General Orde Wingate – as new combat experience was absorbed. Unfortunately for historians, no formal written LRP manuals were ever compiled, printed and disseminated by the HQ of Special Force laying down an authoritative doctrine. Instead, new Chindit officers, NCOs and men relied upon lectures and typed training instructions, memoranda and various draft manuals to learn about this new form of warfare. The 'stronghold' concept, for example, was only laid down in a detailed training instruction issued shortly after Operation *Thursday* began, while 16th Brigade was making its long approach march from Assam. This contained detailed instructions, as well as several diagrams demonstrating the layout of these defensive positions that henceforth formed a central plank of LRP doctrine. The men of the Chindits, moreover, drew and built upon a growing body of written doctrine about the jungle and the Japanese in the form of a series of manuals dealing with conventional jungle fighting produced in India Command from 1942 onwards, including *Military Training Pamphlet No. 9 (India): The Jungle Book* that was widely read and acted upon in training by both Chindits and the rest of India Command and 11th Army Group.

The top diagram shows a Chindit column moving in 'snake' formation through the jungle, c. 1943. The column would move in single file through the jungle either cutting its own path or along an animal track. Each sub unit would have its own first-line mules. The units are: (**1**) rifle platoon (rearguard), (**2**) rear column HQ, (**3**) second-line mule transport and escorting rifle platoon, (**4**) commando platoon, (**5**) support platoon (medium machine guns and 3-inch mortars), (**6**) reserve platoon, (**7**) advanced column HQ, (**8**) Burma Rifles.

The middle diagram shows the leading part of a Chindit column carrying out a 'jig' to disguise its path. (**1**) Individual Chindits turn left and advance on a broad front. (**2**) Individual Chindits move 200–300 yards carefully concealing their tracks behind them. (**3**) Chindits turn right and move off in a column 'snake' along a new axis of advance. (**4**) The advance guard continues half a mile along the original path before doubling back and rejoining the rear of the column.

The bottom diagram shows a Chindit stronghold. (**A**) Stronghold HQ dug-out. (**B**) Stronghold WT dug-out. (**C**) Main personnel sanctuary trenches and dug-outs. (**D**) Stores sanctuary dug-outs and trenches. (**E**) Bays for aircraft sanctuary; bays dug in. (**F**, **G**, **H**) Company area organized in three or four platoon strongpoints, dug in with communication trenches, mined areas and tactical wiring. (**J**) Four 25-pounders mainly sited to defend approaches to the airstrip. Dug in with alternative positions and dummies. (**K**) Anti-aircraft 0.5-inch machine guns or Oerlikon AA guns. (**L**) Keep.

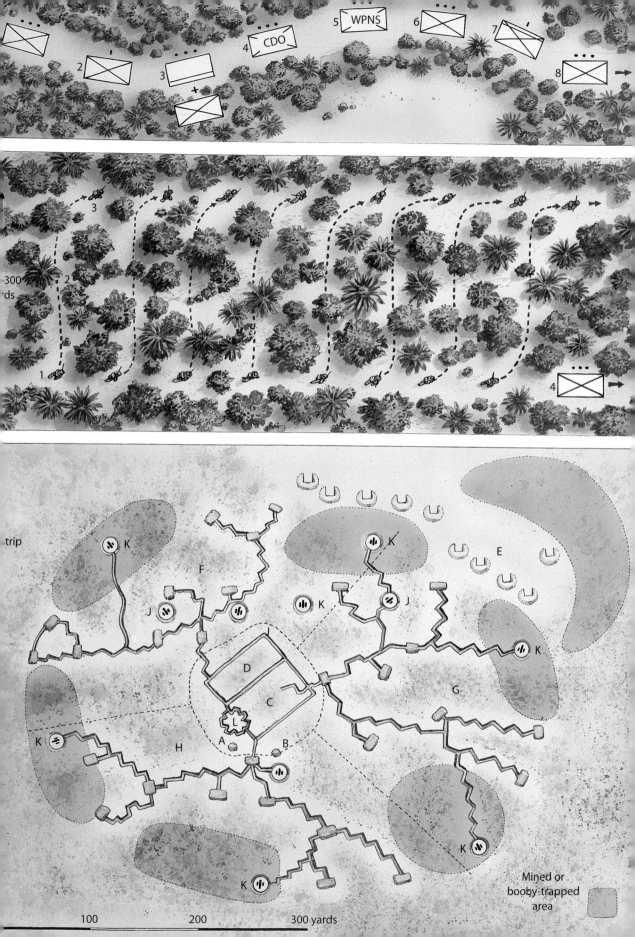

300
yds

1
2
3
4

trip

K
F
J
K
J
K
K
K
J
D
C
L
A
B
H
K
E
K
K
K
G

K

Mined or
booby-trapped
area

100   200   300 yards

An RAF transport parachuting supplies to Chindits in hazardous, hilly jungle territory behind enemy lines. (KY 471207)

skills and taking evasive action by dispersing into small groups and regrouping at prearranged rendezvous points. A lack of knowledge of making river crossings on Operation *Longcloth* meant far greater attention was paid to swimming, improvising boats from local materials, working outboard motors, using toggle ropes, and the handling of infantry assault boats. In particular, the troops of 70th Division needed training in handling mule transport, since it had relied on motor transport before, with officers and NCOs attending General Headquarters (GHQ) Schools and cadres before themselves passing on instruction to newly designated muleteers.

The centrality of airpower to Long Range Penetration was clearly acknowledged during the training of Special Force, with the greater availability of fighter-bomber and bomber aircraft for air support, transport aircraft for air supply and lastly light aircraft for casualty evacuation, greatly facilitating instruction; nearly all of these came from No. 1 Air Commando. Morale was greatly enhanced after watching aircraft practise close air support using live bombs, and the fact that light aircraft demonstrated the ability to evacuate casualties from hurriedly constructed landing grounds. Troops were trained in preparing landing grounds and in receiving supply drops, with such operations controlled by newly allocated RAF wireless sections.

The training period for Special Force culminated as before in a series of large-scale exercises, fully testing its marching powers, as well as practising the coordination of LRPGs by the HQ of Special Force in particular. In many respects the training carried out was debilitating and exhausting, with many men falling ill or being otherwise incapacitated and as a result leaving Special Force. Arguably, during the subsequent operations officers and units who had come late to the Chindits were in far better physical shape than those who had undergone extensive training since 70th Division began conversion to LRP.

BELIEF AND BELONGING

Those officers, NCOs and other ranks who served in the Chindits very quickly became convinced that they belonged to an elite. This deeply held view, with a direct concomitant of giving the new LRP formation as a whole very high morale, owed much to its leader – Major-General Orde Wingate – who in July 1942 faced a very uphill task in preparing his new command for battle. When 77th Indian Infantry Brigade was formed, morale in India Command was at rock bottom. A succession of disastrous defeats in Malaya and Burma in 1941 and 1942, widespread belief that the Imperial Japanese Army were unbeatable jungle fighters, and questioning amongst British other ranks about whether defending India was a worthwhile task, had become deeply entrenched.

The eccentric and highly charismatic Wingate, who possessed a great gift of inspiring the officers and men under his command, quickly improved morale and instilled a new drive and energy amongst his followers, as well as a new sense of purpose. A combination of his personal eloquence, Biblical inspiration and intense belief in his own leadership and ideas meant Wingate exuded sufficient zeal, enthusiasm and quiet confidence to quickly win over those who heard him speak. In part the distinctive and rather eccentric figure he cut in his long-outdated Wolseley sun helmet, scruffy crumpled jungle bush jacket and trousers, dirty boots and rifle hung over his shoulder was a deliberate affectation or piece of showmanship, contributing to his appeal to many other ranks and marked him out as being very different to other senior officers. So did his evident dislike of military formality and personal eccentricities – evidenced by his fervent advocacy of eating raw onions as a health tonic and his lack of concern about greeting fellow officers in the nude. While a small hardcore of Officers remained sceptical of the man, his methods and his ideas, Wingate's compelling magnetic personality and dynamism convinced the vast majority that they could win and make a real difference in the war in the Far East. Indeed, he quickly breathed life and fire into this new force. It has endured to the present day, as witnessed in the vigorous

A close-up shot of a bearded Chindit and his faithful mule during Operation *Thursday*. (SE 7953)

defence of any criticism levelled against their former leader by those who served with the Chindits. Other factors contributed to the high élan and combat effectiveness of the Chindits. Wingate built the Chindit identity upon the firm foundation of the peculiarly British regimental system, in which each British/Gurkha unit possessed a powerful, fiercely defended sense of being an elite drawn from a particular regional area and jealous of its hard-won traditions, beliefs and history. The ultimate bedrock of belief and belonging for all Chindits in large part was to each soldiers' own mates or peer group, with whom he lived, moved and shared basic friendship and mutual support. A sense of being special was inculcated by the arduous training regimen, moreover, that 77th Indian Infantry Brigade undertook, and the fact that so many men were weeded out, with only the best being retained.

The sense of being a special elite, capable of defeating the Japanese 'superman' and living, moving and fighting in the jungle, was cemented amongst officers and men of 77th Indian Infantry Brigade as a result of Operation *Longcloth*. This powerful self-belief, loyalty to and confidence in Wingate and his methods was passed on to the new intake – the officers, NCOs and men of 111th Indian Infantry Brigade, already under training, 3rd West African Brigade and then the brigades of the former 70th Division, by a variety of means. A combination of personal visits, speeches and other pep talks by Wingate and his disciples passed on the message to the new intake, most of whom already had earlier combat experience in North Africa. Morale amongst Chindits under training also soared as a result of skilful propaganda and widespread publicity given to Wingate and his command. A growing sense of corporate identity and a feeling of belonging was magnified, moreover, by the adoption and increasing use of the distinctive name 'Chindit' for LRP troops, a new Chinthe emblem as a formation sign and a Chindit shoulder flash proudly worn on the sleeve of uniforms. Wingate further built upon a bedrock of new propaganda promulgated in India Command during 1943 and 1944, intended to convince British, Gurkha and Indian soldiers of the vital importance of defending India and defeating the 'evil' Imperial Japanese Army, as well as improvements in welfare and living conditions for all ranks. As a result, the

General William Slim, General Orde Wingate and assorted staff officers hold a meeting at Imphal in March 1944. In the background is a B-25 medium bomber. (MH 7881)

majority of Chindits in Special Force went into battle in 1943 and 1944 firmly convinced of the merits of LRP and with the fullest confidence in Wingate's leadership.

The Chindits' high morale – perhaps surprisingly – was maintained during Operation *Thursday*, despite the privations experienced by most of the men. A downside of this profound belief and unquestioning faith in Wingate, however, was the immense psychological shock when news of his death on 24 March 1944 in a plane crash reached Special Force and reverberated down the chain of command. It was felt as a body blow to many men. Arguably the powerful sense of self-belief, the sense of belonging to an elite and high morale enjoyed by the Chindits kept it in being and allowed the unit to weather the storm, despite living, moving and fighting under conditions of extreme hardship and for an extended period of time. A shared experience of marching on foot long distances across difficult terrain, carrying a crushing weight and existing on meagre rations, as well facing the same dangers created an enduring powerful esprit de corps to the end.

The irrepressible Major Bernard Fergusson pictured shortly after Operation *Longcloth*. (KY 471212A)

APPEARANCE, EQUIPMENT AND WEAPONRY

Those troops serving in 77th Indian Infantry Brigade between February and May 1943 largely wore the same tropical uniform on Operation *Longcloth* as other Commonwealth troops in India Command, since specialized lightweight clothing, arms and equipment specifically adapted to living, moving and fighting in a hot, humid and harsh jungle environment was unavailable.

The different units making up 77th Indian Infantry Brigade wore a mixture of kit on their first campaign behind Japanese lines. In February 1943 the soldiers of the 13th King's Regiment entered battle wearing a mixture of hastily re-dyed, Indian-made khaki drill, as well as a few items of locally made, jungle-green dyed uniform and equipment. Headgear consisted of the distinctive, popular and highly practical Australian bush or slouch hat, an item which was both cool and provided shaded vision. Many carried woollen cap comforters to wear at night in higher, colder areas along the Indo-Burmese frontier. Each soldier wore a khaki drill shirts and long trousers, standard heavy ammunition boots and sometimes web anklets. Lightweight woollen pullovers were also carried. In contrast, the Gurkhas and men of the 2nd Burma Rifles wore normal regimental uniform of green-dyed khaki shirts and trousers, web anklets, black leather boots with iron-studded soles and heels and Gurkha hats with a camouflage net.

The Chindits normally entered battle festooned like a Christmas tree with arms, packs and web equipment. Much personal equipment and ammunition was carried, crammed into standard 1937-pattern webbing equipment that had been dyed green just before *Longcloth* began. The basic web ammunition

A group of British, Gurkha and West African troops destined for Burma await the boarding of transport aircraft. (EA 20832)

pouches, worn at the front, contained one four-second No. 36 grenade and 50 rounds of .303 SAA or five 20-round magazines of .45-calibre ammunition depending on the personal weapon issued. In addition, disposable bandoliers of ammunition were often carried draped around the person, as well as a canvas chagal (container) filled with drinking water. A small haversack, a filled bottle and kukri, machete or Dah were also carried on campaign. Overall the arms, webbing, clothing, water bottle and other equipment carried on the person came to about 50 pounds in weight.

The majority of rations, clothing and equipment making up the very heavy load carried by each Chindit on campaign was carried in a steel-framed Everest backpack, designed to keep the weight off a man's back when worn. Although selected as the best equipment for all of 77th Indian Infantry Brigade, they were, however, primarily worn by British troops. In contrast, the Gurkhas in the 3/2nd Gurkha Regiment preferred the ordinary army pack. Each pack normally contained, for example, two pairs of socks, a pullover, mess tin, eating utensils, a 'housewife' containing needle and thread, chlorinating tablets, anti-mosquito ointment, a light-weight blanket, PT shoes, a cap comforter, spare laces, water-wings and toggle ropes. In addition seven days' rations were carried, which made up by far the heaviest weight. Burmese troops also carried 'native' costume – *longyis* (loose robes) – for reconnaissance missions.

The Chindits always carried an extremely light scale of personal weapons and ammunition, similar to that carried by other British troops, as befitted their light infantry role. Between 1942 and 1944 the Chindits largely employed British standard infantry weapons, including the bolt-action .303 Short Magazine Lee-Enfield rifle with long sword bayonet, the US-manufactured .45-inch Thompson submachine gun and the bipod-mounted .303 Bren light machine gun. Initially, the .38 revolver formed the only sidearm issued to Chindit officers, but some US Colt .45-calibre automatic pistols, with a seven-round magazine, were later issued. A range of edged weapons equipped Chindit soldiers for hand-to-hand close-quarter combat – though they were more often used for cutting paths or clearing jungle foliage – including Gurkha kukries, dahs (a Burmese knife) and machetes.

The tried and tested venerable Short Magazine Lee-Enfield Rifle Mk III, originally introduced into British service in 1907, was standard issue for the Chindits between 1943 and 1944. With an effective range of up 3,000 yards, this highly accurate, rugged and extremely reliable weapon was probably the finest manually operated bolt-action rifle in the world. With a muzzle velocity of 2,440fps, its .303 round had great stopping power. Although only having a ten-round magazine, in skilled hands a higher rate of fire was achieved of up to 15 rounds a minute. A long sword bayonet for this weapon was also carried.

The Thompson submachine gun, or 'Tommy gun', was capable of providing a devastating volume of fire at short range. It became a weapon of choice for many Chindits given its spread of fire and great stopping power. A far higher proportion of these weapons were carried than compared to conventional units, normally issued to NCOs. Instead of drum magazines prone to jamming, more reliable 20-round box magazines were employed that were also easier to carry in web equipment.

The Chindits carried the highly effective .303-calibre gas-operated Bren light machine gun. This weapon provided the main source of portable firepower at section level, and was capable of firing single rounds or full automatic bursts. Based on a Czech design developed at Brno and later manufactured at Enfield (hence the name), this extremely reliable automatic weapon weighed in at 23 pounds and was fitted with a bipod for greater accuracy at ranges up to 600 yards. With a magazine containing 30 rounds, the Bren required a crew of two to operate it – one to fire the weapon and a second to carry further containers filled with ammunition, tools, and spares. Several Bren guns were carried in each section and with a practical rate of fire of 120 rounds a minute it was a useful and highly accurate source of firepower.

The different types of grenade used during the Chindit campaigns included the No. 36 Bomb or Mills Bomb, No. 69 concussion grenade and No. 77 phosphorous grenade; the latter was used to produce a smoke screen, but also useful for starting fires or clearing buildings or bunkers. Depending on the individual, No. 36 grenades could be thrown a distance of around 25 yards

A Waco glider lands in central Burma, causing debris to fly in to the air. (SE 7939)

The Chinthe emblem, chosen as the formation sign for the Chindits. (Kevin Lyles)

and were highly effective. Fitted with a discharger cup and firing a ballistite cartridge, special SMLEs, moreover, were retained to fire No. 36 grenades up to 200 yards.

The main source of immediate, close-quarter, indirect fire support at the disposal of Chindit columns was the 2-inch mortar, firing smoke, high-explosive and illumination rounds. This highly effective lightweight weapon consisted of little more than a short tube, a simple firing mechanism and a base plate. It was operated hand-held with the spade or base plate resting firmly on the ground. A round was fired by dropping the shell down the short barrel, after which the angle readjusted for the next shot. It had a maximum range of 500 yards, although for reasons of accuracy it was best operated at a range of 300 yards or less.

Early in the war the bolt-operated 0.55-inch Boyes anti-tank (AT) rifles provided the Chindits with a man-portable anti-armour weapon. Its heavy weight (36 pounds), length (72 inches), limited effectiveness against all but the most lightly armoured vehicle and powerful recoil when fired made it an unpopular weapon from the start. The Boyes AT rifle was normally fired from the prone position, and was employed against tanks, enemy motor vehicles, bunkers and emplacements.

The Chindits' main source of sustained fire support came from crew-served weapons in the form of the venerable, but still highly effective and reliable, water-cooled .303 Vickers medium machine gun and 3-inch mortars; two of each were retained within each column. The tripod-mounted, belt-fed .303 Vickers MMG was capable of producing a greater volume of sustained small-arms fire than any other infantry weapon. It could fire at a rate of up to 500 rounds a minute, directly or indirectly, at ranges up to 3,000 yards, but was extremely heavy at 88.5 pounds. It was operated by a two-man crew – one man to fire the weapon and a second to ensure the smooth feeding of its ammunition belt. Four men and several mules, however, were needed to move the gun, its tripod, ammunition, spare parts and the water needed to cool it.

Three-inch mortars could fire smoke and high-explosive bombs at high trajectory into enemy positions. The mortar consisted of a hollow tube with a firing pin at its bottom, a bipod stand and heavy base plate to absorb recoil.

D   **CHINDIT WEAPONS**

Few of the personal weapons carried and employed by the Chindits during operations *Longcloth* and *Thursday* had been specially developed for use in the jungle. In fact the vast majority were standard tried and tested venerable British infantry weapons that had widely employed in other theatres of war. The simplicity and robustness of the .303 Short Magazine Lee-Enfield rifle (**1**, shown with bayonet), Bren Light Machine Gun (**2**), and to a lesser extent Thompson Submachine Gun (**3**), however, stood the Chindits in good stead during both operations *Longcloth* and *Thursday*, especially during the latter's final phase when the monsoon imposed the greatest test of both men, weapons and equipment. During this period rain and mud posed a constant problem to the operation of these weapons. Only two new personal weapons – the Sten gun (**4**) and small numbers of the US M1 Carbine (**5**) – made their appearance during Operation *Thursday*, with the latter proving highly popular. Although the Sten was much lighter than the Thompson it never escaped an early reputation for being liable to discharge when dropped or mishandled. For heavy support the Chindits were dependent on the .303 Vickers medium machine gun (**6**) and 3-inch mortar (**7**), both of which could be transported, broken down in smaller parts, by mule. During Operation *Thursday* they were supplemented by a small number of Lifebuoy flamethrowers (**8**) – named after the distinctive round fuel tank – that proved highly effective against Japanese bunkers and occupied buildings. The other items shown are a 2-inch mortar (**9**), which weighed 32.5 lb, the Projector, Infantry, Anti-Tank (PIAT) weapon (**10**), the Boys anti-tank rifle (**11**), the Enfield .38 Mk 1 pistol (**12**) and the No. 36 hand grenade or Mills bomb (**13**).

This comparatively crude heavy weapon could be broken down and manhandled in three loads, but on campaign needed several mules to transport it and its ammunition. A major drawback was that each bomb weighed 10 pounds. With a range of up to 1.5 miles and a maximum rate of fire of 15 rounds a minute when used by a well-trained crew, it was a powerful source of indirect fire and constituted the main piece of indirect fire support available to Chindit columns. One major drawback, though, was that it consumed ammunition at a prodigious rate.

The overall weight of arms and equipment carried by each Chindit was crushing, almost bending him double and dominating his life in the field. When fully loaded, Chindit packs and personal equipment weighed in at around 70 pounds on average – about half a man's normal body weight. Following supply drops this weight was often increased further, until rations had been eaten away. Intense rainfall also increased the weight carried, as uniforms and equipment became sodden. Some variations, however, existed, depending on the task allocated to a Chindit. The No. 1 of a Bren gun team, for example, carried 86 pounds just after a supply drop had provided five days' K rations. The weight carried fell to 15 pounds for a brigadier and the relatively few technicians, whose equipment was carried by mules or chargers.

The greatest change in appearance of Chindit soldiers on campaign between 1943 and 1944 on Operation *Thursday* was the far more serviceable jungle-green uniform worn by officers, NCOs and other ranks that was a product of growing British experience of living, moving and fighting in the jungle. For the majority of British and West African troops, this consisted of an Australian bush or slouch hat, an Indian-made grey-green wool flannel, khaki drill or Aertex bush shirt (essentially a four-pocket jacket) worn outside the trousers, cotton battledress trousers and ammunition boots sometimes worn with short puttees. A silk 'panic map' of Burma was normally worn around the neck for use in an emergency. Green-dyed 1937-pattern web equipment, containing a water bottle, ammunition and other personal equipment, was worn as before. On the right hip a kukri was worn covered with a green cotton cover. An Everest pack was worn on the back, normally containing items such as seven days' K rations, a jumper, cap comforter, a green light wool blanket cut in half, a groundsheet, two spare pairs of socks, laces, a housewife, anti-mosquito ointment, mepacrine tablets, toothbrush, toothpaste, razor, soap, a small khaki hand towel and PT shoes.

The same basic mix of small arms – .303 Lee Enfield Rifles, Tommy guns, and Bren guns – were carried by Chindits during Operation *Thursday*, although two new weapons made an appearance. Some officers carried the short, lightweight .30 US M1 carbines, capable of firing semi-automatic from a 15-round magazine – which proved highly popular. Although Thompsons were retained in use until the end of the war, a growing number of the far simpler and cheaper mass-produced Sten machine carbines were carried in the field. Firing a 9mm bullet, this weapon had a 32-round magazine. Although early models had a (thoroughly deserved) poor reputation with regard to safety and reliability, those produced later during the war generally performed well.

The Boyes AT Rifle was replaced between 1943 and 1944 with the PIAT (Projector Infantry Anti-Tank); this weapon fired a hollow-charge round that

A heavily loaded mule is led up a freshly cut path up a hillside. (SE 7927)

was effective up to 100 yards against all Japanese armour and also bunkers. Its only drawback was the heavy weight of its bombs (2.5 pounds each), which meant only a limited number was carried by its two-man crew.

The Lifebuoy flamethrower, worn on the back and, as the name implies, resembling a piece of life-saving equipment, was also employed during Operation *Thursday*. A heavy and cumbersome weapon at best, it proved difficult to load and carry on mules. Although useful against bunkers, the Lifebuoy was loathed both by the Japanese and the unfortunate British troops who employed it: the latter were normally quickly singled out by enemy return fire.

The uniform and equipment of Chindits on both Operation *Longcloth* and Operation *Thursday* rapidly deteriorated while on campaign, and the physical appearance of individual soldiers, suffering from malnutrition and exhaustion, as well as the testing climate and environment, fared likewise. At the discretion of a unit's commanding officer, permission was granted for soldiers not to shave on both Chindit campaigns. Although this did not directly affect many Gurkhas or young soldiers, by the end of the fighting many men sported ragged beards and, given the length of time on active service, shaggy haircuts that would normally cause a regimental sergeant-major to have a coronary. A combination of extremely hard wear and tear incurred during long marches through dense jungle and combat conditions, all the while in moist tropical heat or pouring rain, meant uniforms – especially fabric, webbing and leather items – rapidly tore, fell apart, lost shape, rotted or mildewed. Valiant efforts using needle and thread helped stave off final disintegration, but ultimately could not prevent it. Although replacement uniforms, including new boots (already worn in before the campaign began), were periodically air dropped, this did not meet with demand, and given the curtailment of re-supply missions during the monsoon many men wore little more than sodden, mud-covered rags by the end of Operation *Thursday*. A deadly combination of physical exhaustion, poor diet, disease and the appalling monsoon weather quickly took a heavy toll on the physical appearance of the solders themselves. In particular, the low calorific value of the food provided for both *Longcloth* and *Thursday* meant men became increasingly weak, drawn of face and emaciated as the campaigns progressed.

LIFE ON CAMPAIGN

The life of a Chindit during Operation *Longcloth* was extremely tough, characterized by long, gruelling marches, intermittent fierce fighting and living under extremely difficult conditions deep in the Burmese jungle. A nearly identical experience was shared by troops who participated in Operation *Thursday*. Although the 1944 operations began with a fly-in using gliders and transport aircraft (with the exception of 16th Brigade, which marched in from Assam) – the largest Allied airborne operation to date – this concession to the 20th century quickly ended, with long jungle marches at the pace of the heavily laden mule the norm. The threat of an encounter with Japanese forces hung permanently over the heads of all ranks throughout, with strict military precautions observed at all times. However, for many Chindits combat, either during hit-and-run operations or, in 1944, the defence of strongholds, was quite rare, with much time spent in marching and countermarching and collecting food and fodder for pack animals.

The Burmese jungle formed the backdrop to everyday life. While training in India Command helped familiarize officers and men with conditions of often unsurpassed natural beauty, for most British troops the jungle still remained a strange and often forbidding environment. The combination of its occasionally eerie silences, limited vision, dense vegetation that made movement slow and difficult and a sense of isolation it often instilled were unnerving. Although the sights and sounds of the abundant exotic flora and fauna captivated many, in some respects both posed a threat to the unwary. The Burmese jungle abounded with animal and insect life demanding special precautions, including a variety of biting pests – leeches, mosquitoes and ticks in particular – that formed vectors for disease. By far the mosquito was the most serious threat to life, with malaria causing far, far greater casualties than enemy action, especially since preventative medical arrangements in the Chindits were lax. The onset of the monsoon during the 1944 operations brought with it a raft of new problems for troops, exacerbating existing difficulties and adding new ones for men who were almost permanently soaked to the skin and who had to live, move and fight in a dripping wet jungle, where leeches abounded and the incidence of tropical diseases increased.

The early morning 'stand to', which took place after a night of often poor, fitful sleep in the Burmese jungle within a hurriedly improvised shelter, cramped fox hole or shell scrape, began each day for the Chindit. All men, fully armed, equipped and ready, had to occupy alarm posts for this ritual. A frenetic period of preparation for the day's march immediately followed, with mules requiring feeding, saddling and then careful loading to prevent galls and valuable loads falling off. For all ranks webbing and packs had to be hurriedly loaded and hefted into place on the back, and then troops assumed their designated position in their column's line of march. All traces of the

A group of Chindits and a pack mule advancing along a dusty road. (SE 7929)

A group of P51 Mustang fighter-bombers fly low over Hailakandi airfield, while a B-25H medium bomber taxis into dispersal. These two types of aircraft in No. 1 Air Commando provided close air support to the Chindits, often with pin-point accuracy. (EA 20833)

bivouac area would be carefully removed, with fires and rubbish carefully buried. Some columns breakfasted before departing, while others did so half an hour after leaving the bivouac alongside the track, to make the best of the cool early morning conditions.

The food eaten by Chindits during periodic halts on the march and in bivouacs each day – breakfast, lunch and dinner – had limited appeal at best, and in the long term did little to restore energy, bolster health and improve morale, especially to men continually exerting themselves. During Operation *Longcloth* the staple ration consisted of 12oz Shakapura biscuit, 2oz cheese, 1oz milk powder, 9oz raisins and almonds, 4oz sugar, a tiny allowance of acid drops or chocolate, salt – which was all washed down with tea and accompanied with the inevitable cigarettes. It proved grossly inadequate given how much Chindit soldiers exerted themselves. The widely acknowledged deficiency of these rations led to the adoption of new US foodstuffs for Operation *Thursday* – the 'K ration'. Each daily K ration consisted of three packs (roughly the size of a book), marked breakfast, dinner and supper, all of which could be eaten hot or cold. To facilitate cooking, all had a waxed inner wrapping that burnt easily. Breakfast consisted of instant coffee, powdered milk, a tin of cheese flecked with ham, biscuits, sugar and a date bar. The dinner pack contained lemonade powder, tinned spam, biscuits, chocolate and a fruit bar. Supper was similar fare, with soup powder replacing the lemonade. Four cigarettes were included in each pack, as well as toilet paper. The dearth of tea proved a major sticking point for British soldiers on campaign, however, and tea, powdered milk and sugar were issued as a supplement.

The appeal of K rations – initially a wonderful innovation to those used to British compo or iron rations – quickly paled as one week gave way to another. The normal ways of preparing them soon became unappetising, leading to considerable experimentation, with many preferring a 'porridge' made by mixing all the ingredients together. By the end of the 1944 campaign the K ration was universally hated. As one officer described:

> In Burma we liked it for the first 20 days, tolerated it for the next 20, and for the remaining 100 days loathed the sight of every packet. With very few exceptions, it formed our only meal for five, long, hungry months. (*Thompson 2002, p.170*)

As a result thoughts of food always preoccupied all ranks, and morale suffered accordingly. The most serious drawback by far was that K rations were simply inadequate for the task, failing to deliver sufficient calories for men engaged on arduous operations for long periods of time. The upshot was growing malnutrition, which in turn weakened men who later succumbed more readily to tropical disease. Although supply drops periodically delivered fresh rations, only long periods of rest and plentiful wholesome food (both denied to Chindit columns) could have adequately restored health. The provision of drinking water, moreover, was a problem on both Chindit expeditions. Although plentiful in some jungle areas, quite often troops operated in arid areas where water was marked by its absence. On occasion strict water discipline was required.

The day-to-day experience of Chindit officers, NCOs and men on the march was dominated by hefting the crushing weight of personal arms, webbing and pack (the second and third of which were crammed full of food and other necessities of life) over long distances, up and down through the Burmese hills, under the burning sun or in the airless, deadening heat under a jungle canopy. As one Chindit wrote:

> Setting off in the cool of the morning, the load, though heavy, seemed tolerable, but as the heat and humidity increased the straps of your pack and equipment cut into your shoulders … You tended to lean forward into the weight of your pack and to develop what was known as 'the Chindit stoop'.

As the day progressed the weight of the pack became increasingly unbearable, gradually eroding the endurance and power of thought of men staring fixedly at the back of the man or laden mule in front, increasingly weakened by exhaustion and malnutrition. Sweat poured from every pore in the intense heat and as a result of the heavy weight carried, requiring the addition of salt to water, which was drunk in copious quantities, or simply

A line of bedraggled Chindits march through a Burmese village. (SE 7911)

eaten on its own. As noted previously, during the monsoon months the weight carried increased as water soaked uniforms, webbing, packs and everything within them. As one Chindit described:

> It was then just no longer an oppressive weight but a belted restraint against movement – as though the straps over your shoulder were fastened to powerful springs on the ground and you had to heave up and forward against their pull at every step. *(O'Brian 1984, p. 15)*

Far greater physical exertion, moreover, was required by Chindits marching along paths churned into muddy glissades, in hauling themselves up and then carefully down slippery hillsides and in crossing streams transformed into raging spates. The cumulative result of marching long distances carrying heavy weights, limited and inadequate rations and the exigencies of day-to-day life in the jungle was a growing, debilitating tiredness that bordered on near total exhaustion. Most Chindits went into battle 'absolutely and thoroughly' exhausted before the enemy was even sighted, with a resultant fall in efficiency and morale as the fighting progressed.

The daily march, normally four hours up to lunch and a similar period afterwards, was always carried out in single file or 'column snake' through dense jungle or along animal tracks rather than using existing paths, with the advance guard or 'slashers' moving ahead of the column using dahs, kukries or machetes to cut a path wide enough for the heavily laden mules. Occasionally in more open terrain a column would have flanking patrols out on either side. A column of 400 men and animals would stretch up to a mile in length, with progress and speed dictated by the terrain and type of jungle through which it moved. Each march was carried out in strict silence, with men's eyes fixed on the man or mule in front as they plodded onwards, with jungle closing in claustrophobically on either side. As hundreds of men passed the same way, tracks quickly dissolved into mud, making movement progressively more difficult for man and beast. Mules, weighed down by mortar bombs, small-arms ammunition, radio batteries, charging engines and fuel, frequently fell, collapsed

to the ground under the weight carried or threw their loads. The latter required immediate action by muleteers already working hard at ensuring the free passage of their charges through dense foliage or over fallen trees. A column would often become strung out as minor delays, such as leading mules around or over obstacles, caused it to elongate as the day progressed, with men in the rearguard having to march flat out to keep up.

The threat of Japanese pursuit was always taken seriously, with full military precautions obeyed at all times and great care taken to disguise the path taken by the Chindits. At periodic intervals, columns halted and did a 'jig', with men turning 90 degrees to left or right and then marching a predetermined distance, keeping contact with the man to right or left. Each man would then turn back 90 degrees and resume the march through the jungle on a completely new path. This effectively covered tracks from a pursuing enemy. Every 50 minutes a column normally halted for an eagerly awaited ten-minute break, during which men would throw themselves to the ground for a well-earned rest. The distance covered by a column was extremely variable depending on the going and the physical well-being of the troops. On a march along a road, just under four miles could be achieved by a Chindit column in 50 minutes, but in bad going in the jungle this fell considerably. In Burma on fine days and in good going it averaged about two miles per hour and in mountain and thick jungle it was sometimes down to five miles a day.

The reception of a nightly (and occasionally daytime) supply drop by a column was a frequent and welcome break from normal routine for a Chindit. Indeed, air supply drop was literally the lifeline for Chindits operating behind enemy lines, bringing with it vitally needed food for man and beast, ammunition and other much needed stores, as well as other luxuries. An RAF officer accompanying each column would find a suitable drop zone in the jungle or a clearing whose location was immediately radioed to base. To prevent Japanese interference, platoon ambushes were quickly placed on all likely routes to the area, listening posts sent out on the flanks and in the centre of the DZ another platoon held in readiness for a counterattack. Other troops, meanwhile, quickly collected sufficient fuel for bonfires marking out the landing zone to the air,

A group of Chindits using rubber inflatable boats to cross a wide river in Burma. River crossings were a frequent feature of life on campaign in Burma. (IND 2072)

while others prepared to gather, pile and then redistribute supplies after they were collected. When supplies were dropped by parachute, or free-dropped without them, the contents would be carefully watched as they descended, but even so a considerable amount was often lost. Air re-supply, moreover, had dangers of its own. Injuries caused by air supply drops was known by the generic term 'Death from flying fruit' in 111th Indian Infantry Brigade after a man was killed by free-dropped sack of pineapples. Following the end of a drop, time was of the essence. After supplies were quickly collected, stockpiled and then divvied out, troops would move away for at least half an hour and carefully conceal tracks.

The daily march normally continued until dusk when a column would bivouac in an all-round defensive position. A nightly halting place would normally be located in an area of thick jungle nearby a stream, which provided both drinking water and downstream a site for ablutions and a toilet. A particular drill was followed each day for forming a bivouac, a procedure that had been drummed into each Chindit. When ordered to bivouac, a column

A group of Chindits prepare a roadblock behind enemy lines. (IND 2078)

would do a 90-degree jig and then move into an all-round defensive position in the jungle with the Column HQ at the centre of a rough circle. Several standing patrols would be dispatched into the surrounding area and often an ambush would be carefully laid on the track the column had just been using. For most Chindits the removal and dropping of their pack to the ground was perhaps the favourite time of day, bringing with it a feeling of huge relief and exhilaration. For mule leaders, however, entering a camp was a period of intense activity as mules were unloaded, carefully checked, rubbed down and fed after fodder was collected. The rest of the column would settle down to unload, wash, cook and eat (normally all working in pairs) and improvise shelters from bamboo and other local materials. Noise was kept to an absolute minimum. Each day ended with another 'stand to', after which all men except sentries took off equipment and tried to snatch as much sleep as possible in the stygian gloom. Signal and cipher men, however, continued working long into the hours of darkness.

IN BATTLE

Operation *Longcloth*: No. 3 Column, February–April 1943

No. 3 Column, led by Major Michael Calvert, formed part of 77th Indian Infantry Brigade's Northern Group, when it crossed the Chindwin River at Tonhe on 14 February at the beginning of Operation *Longcloth*. This predominantly Gurkha column consisted of 400 men, 120 mules and a dozen

Operation *Longcloth*, 1943, showing the main routes of advance and retreat.

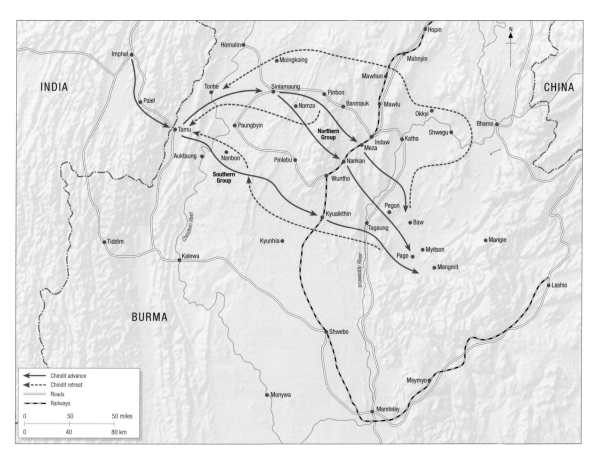

A USAAF L5 light aircraft takes off from a jungle airstrip. (SE 7933)

This picture of Orde Wingate was taken shortly after he returned to Assam after Operation *Longcloth*. (IND 2237)

oxen, the latter providing meat on the hoof and transportation for animal fodder. It slowly advanced over the Zibyu Taungdan Range, after successfully receiving a first supply drop, and then the Mangin Range through an area very thinly occupied by enemy troops. Along with nos. 7 and 8 columns, Calvert was ordered by Wingate southwards to Sinlaumaung where a Japanese force had been reported. No enemy troops were present, however, and they quickly returned to the main body after eating food prepared for the Japanese and liberating an elephant and a horse.

The advance from the Chindwin to the railway line – 100 miles approximately – took roughly two weeks given the difficult terrain that had to be traversed. No. 3 and No. 5 columns profited from diversions made by other columns near Pinlebu, further north, and made direct for the strategically important railway line, running from Shwebo north to Myitkina, to prepare demolitions. When a Japanese garrison was located at Wuntho, direct air support was called in and attacked the village. On 6 March No. 3 Column reached the railway line where it blew up two bridges and destroyed the permanent way in 70 places. Two lorry loads of Japanese infantry coming from Wuntho were ambushed by covering parties protecting the work of the demolition teams, which, after stiff fighting, finally broke contact and fled into the jungle. Without having lost a man No. 3 Column quickly withdrew into the jungle to a prearranged rendezvous, having strewn the surrounding area with numerous booby traps made from 3-inch mortar rounds.

No. 3 Column made slow progress through high elephant grass towards the Irrawaddy River, carefully evading Japanese pursuit. After Burma Rifles patrols discovered that Japanese troops were occupying the small towns of Tigyaing and Tawma,

Calvert carefully slipped between them by night. The Japanese, however, attacked the rearguard just as No. 3 Column began crossing the river, but after abandoning some of its mules and easily replaceable ammunition and medical supplies it crossed with its weapons, wireless sets and explosives. Seven men were killed, however, and six wounded, who were left behind with Burmese villagers. Fortunately, none were harmed during their capture and reached prison safely.

No. 3 and No. 5 columns linked hands four miles south of Hmaingdaing, under the command of Calvert, to begin operations in an area of dry, hot belt of waterless and trackless forest, surrounded by country well served with motorable roads and tracks, far less suited to Wingate's LRP ideas. Increasing difficulties were now encountered by the columns due to growing Japanese activity and the growing exhaustion of both troops and mules from lack of water and being constantly on the move. On 17 March No. 3 and No. 5 columns, operating well ahead of the main body, were ordered to destroy the Gokteik Gorge Viaduct, which carried the road from Mandalay to Lashio (part of the so-called Burma Road). This was the second main objective of Operation *Longcloth* after demolishing the railway, but 150 miles of extremely difficult country lay ahead. The Japanese, moreover, had redoubled their efforts to track the British columns down. No. 5 Column, however, was quickly ordered away to rejoin the main body, leaving Calvert to complete the task with his men. As he advanced towards his objective Calvert set three ambushes to catch a Japanese force patrolling the Nam Mit tributary of the Shweli River. A company of Japanese infantry was caught, and in a particularly one-side action 100 Japanese troops were killed for the loss of

Two officers and NCOs of the Essex Regiment dressed in a mixture of uniform items somewhere in India Command. Note the Chindit formation patch on the shoulder of the NCO on the left of the picture. (IND 4163)

a single Gurkha NCO. On 19 March Calvert received a large supply drop while his exhausted men rested in the nearby hills before marching on Gokteik. However, since No. 3 Column and the rest of the Brigade had reached the limit of practicable air supply, the raid was abandoned, and on these grounds on 26 March Wingate ordered a withdrawal to India.

No. 3 Column was now so far south of the main body of 77th Indian Infantry Brigade that Wingate ordered Calvert to return to India independently. The column moved back towards India stocking up with food from a cache near Baw left earlier during the campaign. Japanese troops were hemming the Chindits in along the Shweli and Irrawaddy rivers, and to the south the situation was also grim. An attempt to cross the Shweli and then either move into China or across the Irrawaddy between Bhamo and Katha failed, leaving Calvert little recourse but to head back towards the Irrawaddy River. A final supply drop was received of food, maps, boots, socks and ammunition before wireless sets, heavy weapons and other items of equipment were destroyed. Shortly afterwards No. 3 Column split up into 10 pre-arranged dispersal groups, which would each proceed independently back to India, in the hope that they would have a better chance of evading the Japanese patrols criss-crossing the jungle in an attempt to hunt them down. In his final report Calvert wrote:

> As soon as all was fixed up all officers, VCOs and GCOs drank a health to the King and Bde in rum at midday, shook hands, and wished each other luck. Then with heavy hearts departed in the various directions, but not very far due to the rum.

As a result the officers and men of No. 3 Column returned to India in dribs and drabs on separate routes, although different groups periodically met and cooperated together. With rations quickly exhausted the dispersal groups relied on locally procured food and what could be foraged from the jungle. Rations were in short supply and drinkable water often difficult to find. En route Calvert carried out further demolitions on the railway, but was then ordered by Wingate to place priority on getting as many experienced men as possible back to India for future operations. Moving at night to escape capture, the Chindits made slow progress. The exhausted, dirty and hungry main body, however, successfully crossed the Chindwin River between Tonhe and Auktang. On 16 April Calvert reached the Chindwin, arriving with the second group of No. 3 Column out of Burma. The majority of his remaining men reached the

 A JUNGLE AMBUSH DURING OPERATION *LONGCLOTH*

The withdrawal to India was by far the most difficult part of Operation *Longcloth*, as, on Wingate's orders, columns broke down into smaller escape groups. With ammunition and food in short supply and the Japanese net tightening day by day the situation was grim. Ahead lay mile after mile of hard marching on short commons through some of the worst terrain in the world, which tested the map reading, will power and endurance of officers and men to the full. En route two wide, fast-flowing rivers had to be crossed either by swimming, aboard hurriedly located country boats or improvised rafts. The Japanese high command, however, were fully alerted to the presence of large numbers of Allied troops moving across their lines of communication and had laid down a cordon to catch as many as possible. As a result many Chindits did not return to cross the Chindwin and fell victim to Japanese ambushes, capture or death from disease or malnutrition en route. This group of NCOs and men from the King's (Liverpool) Regiment, encumbered with the wounded they refused to abandon, is shown at the moment of being caught in a Japanese ambush deep in the Burmese jungle.

A very reluctant mule is pushed and dragged aboard a transport aircraft during Operation *Thursday*. (EA 20831)

Major-General W.D.A. 'Joe' Lentaigne, who assumed command of the Chindits following Wingate's untimely death in March 1944. (IND 3426)

Chindwin weeks ahead of the rest of 77th Indian Infantry Brigade largely as a result of his careful briefing and preparation.

Operation *Thursday*: the capture and defence of White City

77th Indian Infantry Brigade had begun flying into Broadway on 5/6 March 1944. Five Chindit columns led by Brigadier Michael Calvert headed out of the strongpoint soon after, and marched towards the railway valley at Mawlu, along which Japanese supplies were transported to her embattled troops in northern Burma. A series of diversionary attacks, meanwhile, were put in train by two columns drawn from the Lancashire Fusiliers on the railway north and south of the main objective. On 16 March the leading troops – drawn from the 3/6th Gurkha Rifles and 1st South Staffordshire Regiment – reached the small village of Henu, where a cluster of foothills between 30 and 50ft in height, offered a perfect site for a block, dominating both the railway and surrounding area. Several Japanese pickets – occupied by railway engineer and administrative troops – were quickly driven off, although one dominating feature – Pagoda Hill – was initially left undefended by the Chindits. The following day Japanese troops opened up a galling fire from this position as the Chindits continued digging in. A fierce counterattack was launched during the afternoon by a mixed force of British and Gurkhas troops, led by Brigadier Michael Calvert, to eject the Japanese and restore morale. After clearing a nearby hillock, the Chindits raced across the open paddy and up Pagoda Hill. As they approached, the Japanese counter-charged, and a furious hand-to-hand mêlée raged in an area of about 50 square yards with grenades, bayonets, kukris and machetes, and revolvers freely employed

The human cost of long-range penetration was always high. Here a badly wounded Chindit is carried on a stretcher towards an awaiting transport aircraft for evacuation. (SE 7948)

in savage fighting. In the ensuing chaos Lieutenant George Cairns, the South Staffordshire's mortar officer, had his arm nearly severed by a Japanese officer wielding a samurai sword, whom he in turn shot down with a revolver. Despite his left arm being nearly severed, hanging on only by a few strips of muscle, and having been twice bayoneted in the side, Cairns fought on with the captured sword in hand, killing a further Japanese soldier. A final charge cleared the position with the Japanese retreating pell-mell in disorder from Pagoda Hill to Mawlu, after a battle later described as being 'almost medieval in savagery'.

A medical officer administers aid to a wounded Chindit deep behind Japanese lines. (SE 7949)

Chindits hard at work flattening an area of dry paddy for a light-plane airstrip. (SE 7956)

It was the first real battle of the second Chindit campaign, costing 23 killed and 64 wounded. Unfortunately Cairns did not survive for long, and shortly afterwards succumbed to his wounds. For his leadership, bravery and self-sacrifice to his men, however, this young subaltern was later awarded a posthumous Victoria Cross.

The capture of Henu and the repulse of a series of piecemeal Japanese probing attacks on 18, 19 and 20 March acted as a fillip to morale. It bought Calvert a fortnight's grace, moreover, to reinforce, receive air drops of stores, fortify the block or stronghold with deep belts of barbed wire, mines, and booby traps, and dig bunkers roofed with salvaged railway sleepers. Extensive telephone cables were laid and carefully orchestrated defensive fire tasks arranged for supporting Vickers MMGs and 3-inch mortars. A light-plane airstrip was also quickly constructed on nearby paddy fields alongside the railway for casualty evacuation. White City – so called because of the vast number of white parachutes festooning the surrounding jungle – firmly sat

LIEUTENANT GEORGE CAIRNS, VC

77th Indian Infantry Brigade, commanded by Brigadier Michael Calvert, fought its first action of Operation *Thursday* on 12 March 1944, when its leading elements attacked and pushed away a detachment of Japanese railway and other administrative troops near the strategic railway line at Henu. The Chindits immediately began fortifying a series of small hills overlooking the railway. A nearby hill feature – Pagoda Hill – was occupied by the enemy. The following day the enemy opened fire as the Chindits dug in. A fierce counterattack was launched on the afternoon of 13 March, led by Brigadier Michael Calvert, involving a mixed force of South Staffordshires and Gurkhas to eject the Japanese and restore morale. The men raced across the open paddy and up Pagoda Hill, and as they approached the Japanese counter-charged. A furious hand-to-hand mêlée raged in an area of about 50 square yards with grenades, bayonets, kukris/machetes and revolvers freely employed. In the ensuing chaos Lieutenant George Cairns, the 30-year old South Staffordshires mortar officer, had his left arm nearly severed by a Japanese officer wielding a samurai sword, who he in turn shot down with a revolver. Despite his left arm hanging only attached by a few strips of muscle and having been twice bayoneted in the side Cairns fought on with the captured sword in hand, killing a further Japanese soldier and wounding others. A final charge by the Chindits cleared the position with the Japanese retreating pell-mell in disorder from Pagoda Hill to Mawlu, after an engagement later described as being 'almost mediaeval in savagery'. It was the first real battle of the Second Chindit campaign, costing 77th Indian Infantry Brigade 23 killed and 64 wounded. Unfortunately Cairns succumbed to his serious wounds shortly afterwards. For his leadership, bravery and self-sacrifice to his men, however, this young subaltern was later awarded a posthumous Victoria Cross.

astride Japanese road and rail communications in the railway valley, making it impossible for the Japanese to ignore. As a result, the Japanese high command hurriedly re-deployed its forces. In the interim, Chindit columns acted as eyes and ears, attacked approaching enemy troops and generally made their presence felt in the surrounding area by interfering with road and rail communications.

The Japanese launched their first major attack on White City on the night of 21 March, gaining two footholds in the perimeter. A counterattack by the

South Staffordshires (occupying that sector) soon ejected them, albeit at heavy cost. Fierce fighting continued for two days, but by the 23 March the defeated Japanese had retired to Mawlu. Although casualties were heavy, work on the stronghold continued apace. On 29 March 2-pounder anti-tank guns were flown in, as well as construction equipment to build an airstrip big enough for DC3 transport aircraft, which later delivered six Bofors anti-aircraft guns and a battery of 25-pounders. Following this first attack Calvert adopted an offensive defence, using 'floating' columns to strike back against surrounding Japanese forces, beginning with an attack on Mawlu, which was captured after fierce and costly fighting; he also ordered the mining of roads and blowing of several bridges. The first troops of 3rd West African Brigade began arriving to free up 77th Indian Infantry Brigade for operations elsewhere, and took over part of the perimeter.

The Japanese had not been idle, meanwhile, bringing up a motley collection of units from all over Burma (the equivalent of a division) that were placed temporarily under the command of 24th Independent Mixed Brigade. This unit established itself on 1 April in and around Sepein and Mawlu. Under the command of Major Hayashi Yoshihide, it was ordered to clear the block and restore vitally needed traffic on the railway line. The Japanese commenced an all-out assault on White City on the night of 6 April 1944, aiming to eliminate the position once and for all, beginning with a heavy bombardment directed against the south-east corner defended by the Lancashire Fusiliers, Gurkhas and the 6th Nigerian Regiment. A series of spirited infantry assaults were made on the perimeter, supported at one point by Japanese medium bombers, all of which were beaten back with heavy loss by massed 3-inch mortars, Vickers MMGs firing on fixed lines and grenades. The Japanese dead were left hanging in droves on the barbed-wire entanglements encircling the perimeter. For the defenders this was just the beginning of a period of pitched battle made worse by the growing stench of putrefaction that enveloped White City. Further fierce fighting followed for 11 days and nights as the Japanese sought to destroy the stronghold, with the daily bombardment by Japanese artillery growing steadily more intense and placing an immense strain on the defenders, especially after a 6-inch mortar with a devastating blast effect was deployed. Two small Japanese tanks were also brought in, but after one fell victim to 2-pounder AT guns the other withdrew. Throughout, British 25-pounders helped break up the assaults, shelled concentration areas and carried out counter-battery work against Japanese guns. A similar role was played by USAAF P51 Mustang fighter-bombers, backed up by B-25 Mitchell medium bombers, whose pilots displayed considerable skill in making pinpoint attacks close to friendly troops manning the perimeter. During lulls in the fighting further flights of transport aircraft brought in West African reinforcements, food and ammunition until Calvert had roughly seven battalions in and around White City. On 17 April the Japanese made their last assault on White

A large supply organization was a vital necessity to pack and dispatch vitally needed supplies for air dropping to the Chindits. (JAR 2178)

A group of Chindits 'brew up' in a jungle bivouac. (IND 2289)

City, during which Hayashi was killed while leading the attack mounted on a white horse. Although the Japanese penetrated the defences they were either killed by machine-gun fire or evicted in fierce hand-to-hand fighting from the position by South Staffs and West African troops.

The defence of White City was by no means purely passive. On 10 April Lentaigne informed Calvert that 3rd West African Brigade, commanded by Brigadier Gilmore, would garrison the stronghold and that henceforth his troops would operate outside the block. With a striking force consisting of the 3/9th Gurkha Rifles, 7th Nigerian Regiment and a recently arrived column of 45th Reconnaissance Regiment (part of 16th Brigade), Calvert began attacking enemy staging and concentration areas, as well as cutting road and rail communications in the vicinity. This striking force initially had mixed success as it attacked the heavily dug-in Japanese near Sepein on 13 April to draw pressure off the block, despite intense close air support and shelling from White City. Further fierce fighting occurred as the Chindits attacked Japanese lines of communications and troops squeezed into an area between

BELOW RIGHT
A group of senior officers, including Orde Wingate, Colonel Frank Merrill and Brigadier Michael Calvert, at Broadway in central Burma. (MH 7873)

BELOW LEFT
Orde Wingate awaits the arrival of transport aircraft at Broadway. (MH 7882)

Operation *Thursday*, 1944

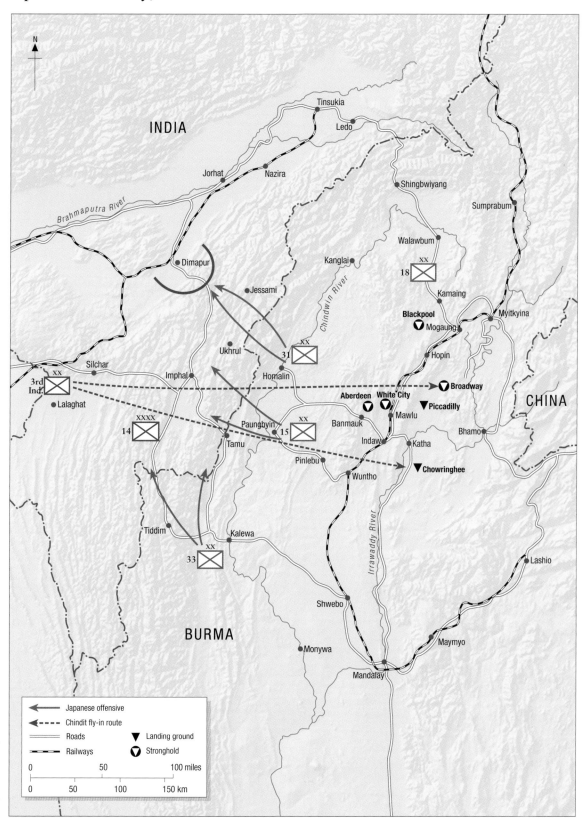

N

INDIA

Tinsukia
Ledo
Jorhat   Nazira
Brahmaputra River
Shingbwiyang
Sumprabum
Dimapur
Walawbum
Kanglai   18 [XX]
Jessami
Kamaing
Ukhrul   31 [XX]
Myitkyina
Blackpool
Silchar   Mogaung
3rd [XX]   Imphal   Homalin
Ind.   Hopin
Lalaghat   Broadway
                                Aberdeen White City
14 [XXXX]   Paungbyin 15 [XX]   Piccadilly
Tamu   Banmauk   Mawlu
                                Indaw   Bhamo
                Pinlebu   Katha
                Wuntho   Chowringhee
CHINA
Tiddim   Kalewa
33 [XX]
Chindwin River
Irrawaddy River
Lashio
Shwebo
BURMA
Monywa   Maymyo
Mandalay

→ Japanese offensive
◄--- Chindit fly-in route
      Roads   ▼ Landing ground
━ ━ Railways   ◉ Stronghold

0   50   100 miles
0   50   100   150 km

51

Calvert and the defenders of White City. Although the Chindits suffered heavily – with nearly 70 dead and 150 wounded – the badly mauled Japanese never attacked White City again.

Now that the menace to White City had been removed, 77th Indian Infantry Brigade reverted to a mobile role and marched northwards on 25 April towards the Gangaw Range. It and its reinforcements had achieved quite remarkable results. A Japanese force of near-divisional strength had been fought to a standstill by seven Chindit battalions – four British, two West African and one Gurkha – and a lengthy break imposed on rail communications. With the centre of gravity of Operation *Thursday* shifting northwards and the monsoon due to close down the airstrip, a decision was taken to abandon White City, along with Broadway and Aberdeen. The final evacuation of the stronghold by 14th Brigade was carried out while the Japanese were still licking their wounds from earlier intense fighting, and proved hugely successful. A succession of DC3s flew in on the final day and night removing casualties, 25-pounders, anti-aircraft and anti-tank guns, stores and other equipment, all of which was back-loaded to India. The heavily mined and booby-trapped fortress was finally abandoned to the enemy on 9/10 May, when the remaining Chindits marched away unopposed northwards to rejoin the main body of Special Force.

Operation *Thursday*: 111th Indian Infantry Brigade and the defence of Blackpool

In early May 1944, 111th Indian Infantry Brigade, commanded by Major Jack Masters, was ordered to establish a new block on the strategic road and railway in the Hopin area, as the centre of gravity of Operation *Thursday* shifted northwards. This new stronghold – codenamed Blackpool – was 60 miles north of White City and occupied an isolated hill feature at the end of a jungle-covered spur running down from the Bumrawng Bum range. It was located near the village of Nawkwin, where it could prevent reinforcements reaching Mogaung and Myitkina and thereby assist Stillwell's NCAC (Northern Combat Area Command) advance. Although not straddling the railway line, the position dominated it from a distance of a mile, had areas defiladed from line of sight, level space for a 25-pounder battery, a good water source and nearby paddy fields where an airstrip could be built. 111th Indian Infantry Brigade was not left unsupported. 14th Brigade, marching north from White City, would protect Blackpool from the west, with the West Africans also in support, while 77th Indian Infantry Brigade would keep east of

Blackpool with the twin aim of protecting the block from that direction and assisting Stillwell's attacks on Mogaung. In some respects, however, the position chosen was far from ideal, especially since it was in close proximity to the forward edge of the battle area in the north, being only 20 miles from a large Japanese garrison at Mogaung, equipped with artillery and heavy weapons.

111th Indian Infantry Brigade was already nearly exhausted when it was ordered northwards, having been in the field for 45 days carrying out hit-and-run attacks in the Japanese rear areas. The already under-strength King's Own and Cameronians occupied the area picked by Masters late on 7 May and overnight began frenzied work building defences. Based on lessons learnt at White City (which Masters had visited), trenches and bunkers were dug, fields of fire cleared, communication cables laid and booby-trapped wire obstacles built surrounding the position. A series of direct fire tasks were arranged for the supporting Vickers MMGs and 3-inch mortars. By far the most urgent task for the initial defence was levelling a landing ground for gliders carrying heavy construction equipment, tools, assorted defence stores and ammunition. As soon as the block was occupied all pack animals were evacuated to Mokso, guarded by the Gurkha No. 30 Column, since they could not be adequately protected below ground from shellfire.

Blackpool came under sporadic Japanese attack almost as soon as it was occupied on the night of 7 May, initially by the outnumbered and outclassed railway troops garrisoning nearby Pinbaw. As a result its defences were never constructed with the same thoroughness as at White City, nor was the position fully stocked with arms, ammunition and supplies for a protracted siege. With supporting floating columns marked by their absence, the Japanese methodically reconnoitred the stronghold, probed the defences, established observation posts and gun positions hidden in the nearby jungle and carefully ranged the position with supporting artillery as it gradually arrived. As a result, the already sick, malnourished and exhausted defenders had little or no opportunity to rest and recover throughout the siege of Blackpool, given the constant digging, back-breaking work parties carrying arms and ammunition up the hillsides, and Japanese attacks at night that interrupted sleep. Using bulldozers and graders flown in by glider from India on 9 May, however, work on a Dakota airstrip quickly began. Desultory shelling by a single Japanese 75mm gun at Pinbaw and probing attacks began the first night the Dakotas landed, attempting to locate British strong points and machine guns on the northern side of the block at a point known as 'the Deep', as well as destroying engineering plant and a damaged C47 on the airstrip. Ominously,

 CHINDIT, OPERATION *THURSDAY*, 1944

The uniform and equipment worn by Chindits during Operation *Thursday* was far better suited to the exigencies of living, moving and fighting in the Burmese jungle than that worn just a year before. In place of hurriedly re-dyed khaki drill, the far more serviceable new jungle-green shirt and trousers was available. These clothes were much lighter, harder wearing and far cooler than those worn before. The webbing equipment worn by all ranks, holding grenades, ammunition, and personal effects, remained, however, generally unchanged, despite the fact that it soaked up water and quickly rotted. A combination of heavy wear and tear, the hot, humid and sticky climate and enemy action, however, quickly reduced even these jungle-green uniforms and webbing equipment to a state of near ruin. With aerial re-supply of new clothing a virtual impossibility during the monsoon months, by the end of the fighting in Burma all Chindits in the field looked dirty, ragged and dishevelled. Disease was widespread, with many Chindits remaining in the field long after they would have normally been evacuated for medical treatment.

the next morning a newly deployed 105mm Japanese guns began harassing fire on Blackpool.

The Japanese maintained heavy pressure on the Deep sector, making a series of head-on attacks repeated every night for five days – largely ignoring other more vulnerable, lightly defended sectors of the perimeter. In particular, the vital airstrip, fully operational from 12 May, where DC3 after DC3 brought in vitally needed supplies and evacuated casualties, escaped attack despite being in full view. These Japanese assaults, moreover, conducted mostly at platoon strength, displayed little skill or subtlety and as a result suffered heavily in the face of intense small arms, MMG and mortar fire. They did, however, gradually wear down the willpower and endurance of the over-worked men of the King's Own. 25-pounders, 2-pounder anti-tank guns, Bofors anti-aircraft guns, ammunition, barbed wire and other supplies, meanwhile, were slowly flown in. As intended the 25-pdr artillery battery began on 13 May bombarding the railway line, supporting the perimeter and abortively trying to suppress the Japanese artillery. Throughout the day USAAF Mustangs and B-25s, called in by the Chindits, wheeled overhead, bombing and strafing suspected enemy positions or concentration areas and giving the attackers no respite. As a result the Japanese kept close to the perimeter to escape air attack, with snipers exacting a heavy toll on the defenders. As time progressed the Japanese artillery grew increasingly bold and employed ammunition on a lavish scale, causing a steady drain of casualties and preventing the defenders from sleeping. On 17 May Japanese 105mm and 155mm artillery and mortars systematically pounded the Deep with such ferocity that Masters was forced to quickly substitute its exhausted garrison for fresher troops. A gap of an hour, however,

A group of West African Chindits board an RAF C-47 Dakota transport aircraft en route for Burma. (IND 7046)

meant that the ensuing and determined Japanese infantry attack failed, being halted early the following morning by intense machine-gun, mortar and artillery fire. However, the next day the Japanese broke contact and withdrew into the jungle to lick their wounds, after suffering heavy losses to air attack and artillery and mortar fire during the course of repeated ground attacks. A Chindit patrol found few Japanese bodies, but the jungle was littered with bloody bandages, empty cartridge cases, and equipment.

The glowering monsoon clouds had steadily built up since Blackpool had been occupied, with rain showers growing steadily in frequency and intensity. When the monsoon finally broke, in its full fury, it had a massive impact on operations in and around the stronghold. As Masters later wrote:

> The Deep sector looked like Passchendaele – blasted trees, feet and twisted hands sticking out of the earth, bloody shirts, ammunition clips, holes half full of water, each containing two pale huge-eyed men, trying to keep their rifles out of the mud. (*Masters 1961, p.245*)

A combination of the pouring rain and limited vision because of dense cloud sharply curtailed air supply missions using the airstrip, preventing the replenishment of food and especially ammunition (which was being consumed at a prodigious rate), as well as interfering with vitally needed close air support. Evacuating the sick and wounded, moreover, became increasingly difficult. The sick rate in Blackpool also soared, with jungle sores and malaria abounding amongst exhausted men already physically debilitated by malnutrition.

The monsoon had perhaps the greatest impact on the Chindit columns advancing towards Blackpool in support, with movement through the dripping

A group of tired and bearded Chindits in 16th Brigade carry a wounded comrade through the jungle. (KY 481781)

wet jungle along slippery muddy paths and tracks slowed to an almost glacial pace. Rivers quickly flooded, overflowing their banks and becoming impossible to cross, while streams and rivulets were transformed into raging torrents. 14th Brigade was bogged down en route to Blackpool by the weather and extremely difficult terrain, and Japanese resistance prevented it being used as floating columns around the stronghold as intended. In large part 77th Indian Infantry Brigade could only watch from the far side of the Namyin River, now in full spate, as the Japanese assault on Blackpool gathered pace and ferocity.

The defenders of Blackpool briefly enjoyed a respite amidst the growing monsoon rains after the attackers on the Deep withdrew. It was none too soon, since both of Masters' original British battalions were near dead on their feet having fought and worked hard for 10 days since the stronghold was occupied. The embattled garrison of Blackpool did receive some support. On 20 May the comparatively fit, fresh and rested 3/9th Gurkha Rifles arrived and took over the southern perimeter, followed by No. 82 Column of the King's Regiment from Broadway. With sufficient manpower now available, the perimeter was thickened and floating columns were sent out from Blackpool into the surrounding jungle to seek out and destroy the Japanese artillery, as well as delay further Japanese troops advancing towards the stronghold.

The progressive arrival of the main body of the Japanese 53rd Division – a second-line, but still a dangerous opponent – in the Hopin area the same day, however, and a rapid deterioration of the weather meant the writing was on the wall for Blackpool. On 22 May the reinforced Japanese 128th Regiment drove back a single Cameronian column trying to delay it, and approached within striking distance of the south-east corner of the embattled perimeter. The Japanese regiment brought with it four more artillery pieces that shelled the airfield, as well as heavy anti-aircraft guns that dominated the sky around Blackpool. Whenever transport aircraft approached the airstrip, after the clouds briefly cleared, the Japanese opened fire, but carefully kept quiet whenever escorting Allied fighter-bombers tried to locate and destroy them. A combination of the direction of the new attack, showing far greater skill than earlier efforts, and the presence of anti-aircraft guns meant only supply drops onto the block itself or on the nearby jungle at night were feasible. As so many loads fell into enemy-occupied areas, however, supplies of ammunition rapidly dwindled.

The Japanese 128th Regiment, newly arrived from Rangoon, attacked the airstrip en masse on 23 May supported by intense shellfire, and, although suffering heavy losses, successfully drove the defenders of the outlying 'Pimple' feature back within the block's perimeter, with the loss of the vital airstrip itself and two hurriedly spiked Bofors anti-aircraft guns. Casualty evacuation was now impossible and heavy cloud and rainfall meant close support and supply dropping was limited. Probing attacks intensified along the eastern face of the block, while intense shelling continued unabated. During the 24 May the Japanese closed in around the southern sector of the block and incessantly shelled and mortared the crumbling defences. It proved the decisive day of the battle for Blackpool. By now conditions within Blackpool were appalling, with

A wounded Chindit is loaded aboard a US L5 Light aircraft for evacuation to India. (SE 7947)

Japanese pressure mounting inexorably. With the defenders nearly exhausted by constant work and fighting, food and ammunition rapidly dwindling and no hope of re-supply or reinforcement, the situation was clearly untenable. With supporting troops from 14th Brigade still far away, moreover, the garrison of Blackpool felt abandoned and morale suffered accordingly. Casualties mounted alarmingly under heavy shellfire and repeated ground assaults, with the MDS (Main Dressing Station) overflowing with the dead, dying and badly wounded. An attempt at air supply ended in disaster when approaching RAF DC3s encountered heavy anti-aircraft fire from guns near the airstrip, and only four out of eight aircraft returned to base. Only half of one aircraft load of ammunition was eventually recovered by the embattled Chindits.

The night of 24/25 May was one of considerable confusion, as Masters carefully reassessed his position. Although casualties had been comparatively light to date within Blackpool for such a desperate defence, ammunition was in critically short supply, making a prolonged defence without outside support impossible. In part the decision was made on 25 May for him. During the early hours the Japanese again broke into the perimeter and seized a small post from the 3/9th Gurkha Rifles overlooking the artillery battery. Following an abortive counterattack launched by the Cameronians, Masters acted on his own initiative while sufficient ammunition remained to break contact, and gave orders at 8.00am to withdraw and keep 111th Indian Infantry Brigade in being as a fighting formation.

The evacuation of Blackpool, amidst driving rain and bursting Japanese shells and mortar bombs and along difficult and slippery, muddy jungle tracks, was masterly executed. For three days the exhausted, shell-shocked and hungry survivors, encumbered by the wounded, slogged their way through the jungle over the Bumrawng Bum to Mokso Sakkan, through successive, skilfully deployed layback positions. Some 130 wounded were evacuated, but those too ill to move were given fatal does of morphia or shot rather than leaving them

Brigadier Michael Calvert directs one of the last operations by 77th Indian Infantry Brigade near Mogaung. The officer to the right is carrying a much sought after US M1 Carbine. (MH 7287)

behind to the Japanese. Fortunately the sick, exhausted and half-starved Japanese 53rd Division made no attempt to halt them, having been fought to a near standstill itself. The 7th Nigerian Regiment met the survivors en route and took over the rearguard, and the survivors of Blackpool reached Mokso on the 27 May.

111th Indian Infantry Brigade had been soundly beaten and had lost heavily in the process, suffering some 210 casualties, but had inflicted large losses on the attacking Japanese. It had fought the sort of conventional battle for which the Chindits had not been adequately trained. Even so, this under-strength formation had successfully blocked the main Japanese line of communication to the north for a fortnight. A heavy price had been paid for locating the block in an area where the 53rd Division, with its supporting heavy artillery, could deploy easily. Unlike at White City the Japanese reaction as a result had been swift, violent and in strength. 111th Indian Infantry Brigade, however, remained in being to fight another day. The Japanese, however, had cleared their line of communication and were free to assist either the garrison at Myitkina or the 18th Division at Kemaing.

THE DEMISE OF SPECIAL FORCE

The officers, NCOs and men of Special Force displayed considerable skill, courage, self-sacrifice and powers of endurance during Operation *Thursday*, just as the original Chindits had done the year before. They had carried out the biggest behind-the-lines operation of World War II to date, involving some 20,000 men, and had lived, moved and fought for five months under appalling conditions against the Imperial Japanese Army, carrying out operations increasingly of a conventional nature. The exhausted survivors, pale shadows of their former selves, required an extended period of leave, rest and recuperation following the end of the campaign in August 1944 when the remnants of 77th Indian Infantry Brigade, 3rd West African and 111th Indian Infantry Brigade finally returned to India. Despite Wingate's strictures and repeated requests for timely evacuation, they had been kept in the field far too long and had suffered accordingly. Very few of the originals remained as a result of battle casualties, the ravages of tropical disease and large-scale repatriation of British personnel, who had been overseas for a long period, to the UK. A major infusion of new blood into Special Force began immediately, since so many survivors were unfit for further service, to rebuild it, and training began for further projected long-range patrol operations in South-East Asia, including a glider-borne landing north of Rangoon. It was not to be, however, with Operation *Thursday* proving the largest and last long-range patrol operation of World War II.

The brief life of the Chindits had come precipitately to an end, as the war in Burma gathered pace following the climactic battles of Imphal and Kohima that broke the back of the Imperial Japanese Army. In February 1945 an assembled group of Chindits was informed that Special Force would be broken up and its units and personnel dispersed to other formations in India Command/Burma. This decision to disband Special Force was greeted with disillusionment and profound shock and dismay by all Chindit veterans, who regarded it as a victory for Wingate's many critics in the Indian military establishment and a stab in the back. Without a champion to fight their corner or direct access to support in high places to defend them following the death

of Wingate, the days of the Chindits were over. To a large extent, however, the disbandment of Special Force was recognition of the dramatic change in the strategic conditions in Burma, as conventional armoured and motorized forces under the command of Lieutenant-General Sir William Slim surged forward across the Irrawaddy River to Meiktila, onwards to Rangoon and to ultimate victory in Burma. Transport aircraft needed to support a major long-range patrol operation, moreover, were now in short supply. The Chindits, quite simply, were no longer needed in the immediate or distant future, and as an acute British manpower shortage affected all units in India Command such a profligate use of resources was now simply an impossibility.

The lessons learnt by Special Force, however, were not forgotten and indeed following its disbandment were successfully passed on, in many respects for the first time, to the rest of British forces in the Far East. A combination of cross-posting of officers, NCOs and other personnel, as well as the transfer of complete units, meant regular units and formations profited from the hard-won experience of Operation *Thursday*. Indeed, by 1944–45 Fourteenth Army as a whole was employing air transportation, aerial re-supply and close air support on a hitherto unprecedented scale, in large part based on methods developed by Wingate and Special Force. As Lord Louis Mountbatten later wrote to Brigadier Michael Calvert:

> It was the most distasteful job in my career to agree to your disbandment.
> I only agreed because by that time the whole Army was Chindit-minded.
> (*Calvert 1996, p. 183*)

The results achieved by the Chindits have been, and will probably always be, a bone of contention amongst the dwindling band of surviving veterans and new generations of military historians. Did the large investment in dead, wounded and sick and other resources occasioned by long-range penetration operations pay a sufficient dividend? In brief the 1943 Chindit operations may have been limited and transitory in effect and cost heavy British casualties, but they also played a key propaganda role, and helped pioneer the aerial supply of large formations and develop other jungle-fighting methods. Indirectly, moreover, Operation *Longcloth* convinced the Japanese high command that an overland invasion of India was possible, which ultimately led to their decisive defeat at Imphal and Kohima. Undoubtedly the Chindits in 1944 had played a significant part in assisting the NCAC's advance down the Ledo Road and the final capture of Mogaung. The contribution Special Force made to victory at Imphal and Kohima (with the exception of 23rd Brigade), however, was far more limited than some historians have claimed, with it only having a very indirect impact on operations. A question mark will always remain over what would have happened had the enigmatic Wingate not died in March 1944, and had his further ideas for long-range penetration been put into effect. Whatever final conclusions are reached, what is unchallengeable is the personal contribution and heroic part played by individual Chindit officers, NCOs, and men. As Julian Thompson has summed up:

> No cold accounting of return on investment can take away what they achieved in personal terms. They truly deserve the standing and the adulation they were accorded at the time, and since. (*Thompson 1998, p.256*)

MUSEUMS, COLLECTIONS AND FURTHER RESEARCH

The main archival repository for documents relating to the Chindits in Burma can be found in the National Archives at Kew in London. This includes policy documents relating to the organization and planning for Chindit operations in the WO 203 series, as well as war diaries and similar documents perhaps of greater interest to the general public. A caveat should be added about the war diaries, however, since they vary greatly in coverage and quality and often the original documents contained in appendices to each monthly report were either not forwarded to the UK or else have gone missing. Most war diaries were written by over-worked intelligence officers, moreover, who could often spare little time on campaign for producing a definitive account of their unit's activities. Elsewhere the main source of information is located at the Imperial War Museum at Lambeth in London. By far the most important source are the papers of Major-General Orde Wingate, which contain a wealth of information about his life and career, including many documents relating to raising, organizing and training the Chindits. The National Army Museum in Chelsea also has some material and displays relating to the Chindits.

The availability of Chindit ephemera with good provenance for collectors is far more limited. Little of the uniform, webbing and other equipment worn by the Chindits on active service has survived the war, given the intense wear and tear imposed by living, moving and fighting in a jungle environment. A combination of rot, mildew and rust meant that most uniforms worn by returning Chindits in 1944 were simply consigned to the fire or the refuse tip. Any items on offer at auction houses or online should be treated with considerable caution. Insignia – formation signs and regimental badges – is perhaps the most widely available of the items relating to the Chindits, but should be treated with considerable care given the large number of fakes and reproductions on the market. Similarly, given the regrettable decision to issue campaign medals without names means that single medals or groups attributed to Chindits should be treated with considerable circumspection unless accompanied by supporting paperwork.

SELECT BIBLIOGRAPHY

Allen, Louis *Burma: The Longest War* (London: Dent, 1984)

Anglim, Simon 'Orde Wingate and the Theory Behind the Chindit Operations',
    Royal United Service Institution Journal, 147, No. 2 (April, 2002), pp. 92–97

—— 'Orde Wingate, Guerilla Warfare and Long-Range Penetration, 1940–44',
    Small Wars and Insurgencies, 17, No. 3 (September 2006), pp. 241–62

Baggaley, James *A Chindit Story* (London: Souvenir Press, 1954)

Bidwell, Shelford *The Chindit War* (London: George Allen & Unwin, 1985)

—— and Mead, Peter 'Orde Wingate: Two Views', *Journal of Contemporary History*, 15
    (July 1999), pp. 401–04

Burchett, W.G. *Wingate's Phantom Army* (Bombay: Thacker, 1944)

Calvert, Michael *Prisoners of Hope* (London: Jonathan Cape, 1952)

—— *Fighting Mad*, 2nd edition (London: Airlife, 1996)

—— *Chindit* (London: Ballantine, 1964)

Carfrae, Charles *Chindit Column* (London: Kimber, 1985)

Chinnery, Philip *March or Die: The Story of Wingate's Chindits* (London: Airlife, 1997)

Fergusson, Bernard *Beyond the Chindwin* (London: Collins, 1945)

—— *The Wild Green Earth* (London: Collins, 1946)

—— *The Trumpet in the Hall* (London: Collins, 1970)

Hedley, John *Jungle Fighter. Infantry Officer, Chidnit & SOE Agent in Burma, 1941–1945*
    (Brighton: Tom Donovan, 1996)

Hickey, Michael *The Unforgettable Army: Slim's XIVth Army in Burma* (London: BCA, 1992)

James, Robert Rhodes *Chindit* (London: John Murray, 1980)

James, Harold *Across the Threshold of Battle* (Lewes: The Book Guild, 1993)

Jeffrey, W.F. *Sunbeams Like Swords* (London: Hodder & Stoughton, 1951)

Jeffreys, Alan *British Infantryman in the Far East 1941–45* (London: Osprey, 2001)

Kirby, Major-General Woodburn (ed.) *The Official History of The War Against Japan*,
    vols. II and III (London: HMSO, 1962 and 1965)

Leathart, Scott *With the Gurkhas: India, Burma, Singapore, Malaya, Indonesia 1940–1959*
    (Edinburgh: Pentland Press, 1986)

Masters, John *The Road Past Mandalay* (London: Micheal Joseph, 1961)

Mead, Peter *Orde Wingate and the Historians* (Devon: Merlin Books, 1987)

Moreman, Tim *The Jungle, the Japanese and the British Commonwealth Armies
    at War, 1945–45* (London: Frank Cass, 2006)

Painter, Robin *A Signal Honour: With the Chidnits and XIV Army in Burma* (London:
    Leo Cooper, 1999)

Rolo, Charles *Wingate's Raider's* (London: Harrap, 1944)

Rooney, David *Burma Victory* (London: Arms and Armour Press, 1992)

—— *Wingate and the Chindits. Redressing the Balance* (London: Arms and Armour Press, 1994)

Royle, Trevor *Orde Wingate* (London: Weidenfeld and Nicholson, 1982)

Sharpe, Phillip *To Be A Chindit* (London: White Lotus Press, 1995)

Shaw, Jesse *The March Out* (London: Hart Publishing, 1953)

—— *Special Forces: A Chindit's Story* (London: Alan Sutton Publishing, 1986)

Slim, Field Marshal Sir William *Defeat into Victory* (London: Cassell, 1956)

Smith, E.D. *Battle for Burma* (London: Batsford, 1979)

Stibbe, Phillip *Return Via Rangoon* (London: Leo Cooper, 1994)

Sykes, Christopher *Orde Wingate* (London: Sykes, 1959)

Thompson, Julian *The Imperial War Museum Book of War Behind Enemy Lines* (London:
    Imperial War Museum, 1998)

—— *The Imperial War Museum Book of the War in Burma* (London: Imperial War Museum, 2002)

Thompson, Sir Robert *Make for the Hills* (London: Leo Cooper, 1988)

Towill, Bill *A Chindit's Chronicle* (London: Author's Choice, 2000)

Tulloch, Derek *Wingate in Peace and War* (London: Macdonald, 1972)

INDEX